An

at your Fingertips

Other titles in this series

Arabic

at your Fingertips

compiled by

LEXUS

with

Adel Ezzeldin and Janet Leng

Routledge
London

First published in 1988 by
Routledge
a division of Routledge, Chapman and Hall
11 New Fetter Lane, London EC4P 4EE

Set in Linotron 202 Baskerville
by Morton Word Processing Ltd, Scarborough
and Computype Ltd, West Drayton
and printed in the British Isles
by The Guernsey Press Co Ltd
Guernsey, Channel Islands

Library of Congress Cataloging in Publication Data

Arabic at your fingertips/compiled by Lexus with Adel Ezzeldin and Janet Leng.
    p. cm.
1. Arabic language – Dialects – Dictionaries – English. 2. Arabic language – Dialects – Egypt –
Dictionaries – English. 3. English language – Dictionaries – Arabic. 4. Arabic language – Dialects
– Egypt – Grammar. I. Ezzeldin, Adel. II. Leng, Janet. III. Lexus (Firm)
PJ6795.A69 1988

                                                                        87-32100

British Library CIP data also available
ISBN 0-415-00235-4

Contents

Introduction

Classical Arabic, the language of the Koran, is the universal *written* language of the entire Arab world. It is quite complex and many native Arabic speakers find it very difficult. It is rarely spoken and should certainly not be encountered by the visitor in his everyday dealings within an Arab country.

Colloquial Arabic is the language *spoken* by Arab peoples. It varies tremendously between countries in grammar, vocabulary and pronunciation although its written form remains constant. The Egyptian variety of colloquial Arabic used in this book is well recognized through the spread of popular films and songs. It is, fortunately, much simpler than Classical Arabic. Indeed a speaker of Egyptian colloquial Arabic will always try to avoid complicated constructions and will attempt to say things in the simplest possible way. English-speakers should find word order and sentence structure fairly familiar.

Egyptians, living as they do at the crossroads of the Middle East, are more than accustomed to hearing a wide variation of speech. You are likely to find every effort made to understand your attempts at the language. This tolerance and the preferred simplicity of Egyptian Arabic should encourage visitors to make a confident approach to the Arabic language from the very beginning of their stay.

THE ARABIC ALPHABET

This table shows the letters of the Arabic alphabet in the different forms they take according to their position in a word. The righthand column is the equivalent English sound as used in the pronunciation system in this book.

Final	Median	Initial	Isolated	
ا	ا	أ ـ ا	أ	a
ب	ـبـ	بـ	ب	b
ت	ـتـ	تـ	ت	t
ث	ـثـ	ثـ	ث	s
ج	ـجـ	جـ	ج	g
ح	ـحـ	حـ	ح	H
خ	ـخـ	خـ	خ	kh
د	ـد	د	د	d
ذ	ـذ	ذ	ذ	z
ر	ـر	ر	ر	r
ز	ـز	ز	ز	z
س	ـسـ	سـ	س	s
ش	ـشـ	شـ	ش	sh
ص	ـصـ	صـ	ص	s
ض	ـضـ	ضـ	ض	d
ط	ـطـ	طـ	ط	t
ظ	ـظـ	ظـ	ظ	z
ع	ـعـ	عـ	ع	*
غ	ـغـ	غـ	غ	gh
ف	ـفـ	فـ	ف	f
ق	ـقـ	قـ	ق	k
ك	ـكـ	كـ	ك	k
ل	ـلـ	لـ	ل	l
م	ـمـ	مـ	م	m
ن	ـنـ	نـ	ن	n
و	ـو	و	و	w
ة	ـهـ	هـ	ة	h
ى	ـيـ	يـ	ى	y
ڤ	ـڤـ	ڤـ	ڤ	v
چ	ـچـ	چـ	چ	SH

Pronunciation Guide

Although written Arabic is the same throughout the Arabic world, there are differences in pronunciation. The Arabic translations in this book have been written in a pronunciation system which reflects the spoken language that you will encounter in Egypt. You will, however, find that this way of speaking Arabic is generally familiar to people throughout the Arabic world largely as a result of films and television. Where a translation is given in quotes this means that the pronunciation is more or less equivalent to the English pronunciation of the word. Where one or two letters are given in bold type this means that this part of the word should be stressed.

VOWELS

a	as in 'cat'		I	as in 'eye' or 'night'
ā	similar to the 'a' in 'cat' but longer		o	as in 'not'
aa	as in 'car'		ō	as in 'moment'
ay	as in 'may'		oo	as in 'boot'
e	as in 'met'		ow	as in 'now'
ē	as in 'pair'		u	as in 'bull'
ee	as in 'meet'		uh	as in 'mud'
i	as in 'sit'			

Arabic vowels should always be pronounced with equal clarity and never swallowed as often happens in English with, for example, the last syllable of 'seven'.

CONSONANTS

h	is always pronounced – except when occurring in the following combinations: gh, kh, sh, sн, th, uh
kh	as in the Scottish pronunciation of 'loch'
p	only occurs in loan words and will be pronounced 'b' by Egyptians
r	must be strongly rolled and never silent as in English
s	as in 'so' or 'hiss', never as in 'advise'
sн	as the 's' sound in 'pleasure'

A double consonant such as 'tt' or 'nn' should be sounded twice – as in Italian.

SPECIAL SOUNDS

gh	as a French 'r'
н	an emphatic 'h'; you should forcibly breathe out from your throat while pronouncing this sound
'	glottal stop; as often heard in regional forms of English when the letter 't' is omitted, as for example in 'ho' wa'er bo'le' for 'hot water bottle'
*	this sound is much more difficult to describe than it is to produce; it represents the letter 'ine' in Arabic; imagine making the classic comic strip scream 'aaaaaagh' straight from your throat; if you can now produce the same sound but very briefly you should be making the right sound; it will become much easier if you do not worry about the sound in isolation; instead try to use it quickly and blend it into any following vowel, usually an 'a', to modify the overall sound

English-Arabic

A

a: 20 piastres a bottle *ashreen uhrsh el ezaza; *see page 102*

about: about 25 Hawālee khamsa wa *ashreen; **about 6 o'clock** Hawālee e-sa*a sitta; **is the manager about?** el modeer mowgood?; **I was just about to leave** ana kunt lessa mashee; **how about a drink?** teshrab ay?

above fō'; **above 5** fō' khamsa

abroad (*go*) lil khareg; (*live*) fil khareg

abscess dimil

absolutely: it's absolutely perfect da tamam awee; **you're absolutely right** inta *ala Ha'; **absolutely!** kuht*an!

absorbent cotton otna tebbee

accelerator dawāsit benzeen

accept mowafi'

accident Hadsa; **there's been an accident** kan fee Hadsa; **sorry, it was an accident** asif ghuhsb *anee

accommodation(s) sakken; **we need accommodation(s) for four** *a-izeen sakken lay arba*a

accurate mazboot

ace (*cards*) uhs

ache: I have an ache here *andee waga* hena; **it aches** bitooga*

across *abr; **across the street** *abr e-shari*a

actor momasil

actress momasilla

adapter (*electrical*) *not generally available — advisable to take your own*

address *inwān; **what's your address?** *inwānak ay?

address book kitab *anaween

admission: how much is admission? e-dikhool bikam?

adore: I adore ... (*this country, this food etc*) ana baHebb ...

adult sheb

advance: I'll pay in advance Hadfa* mō'adam

advertisement e*alēn

advise: what would you advise? inta ra'yak ay?

aeroplane tiyara

affluent baHbooH

afraid: I'm afraid of heights ana bakhef min el *tloo; **don't be afraid** matkhefsh; **I'm not afraid** ana mush khayf; **I'm afraid I can't help you** asif mush Ha'dar asa*duhk; **I'm afraid so** lil asif; **I'm afraid not** la'

after ba*d; **after 9 o'clock** ba*d e-sa*a tis*a; **after you** ba*dak

afternoon ba*d e-dohr; **in the afternoon** fil dohraya; **good afternoon** misē' el kheer; **this afternoon** e-dohraya

aftershave lōshan

afterwards ba*dayn

again mara tania

against duhd

age *omr; **under age** moraahek; **not at my age!** mush fee sinee!; **it takes ages** bitakhud wa't taweel; **I haven't been here for ages** ana magetsh hena min zamān

agency wikāla

aggressive *adwānee

ago: a year ago min sana; **it wasn't long ago** mush min moda taweela

agony: it's agony alam shedeed

agree: do you agree? inta mowafi'?; **I agree** ana mowafi'; **it doesn't agree with me** matwafi'neesh

1

AIDS 'AIDS'

air howa; **by air** bi tIyara

air-conditioning takeef howa

air hostess modeefa gawaya

airmail: by airmail bil bareed e-gawee

airmail envelope zurf bareed gawee

airplane tIyara

airport mataar

airport bus ōtōbees el mataar

airport tax dareebit el mataar

alabaster rokham

alarm inzaar

alarm clock minnabeh

alcohol koHol

alcoholic: is it alcoholic? da koHollee?

Alexandria iskindraya

Algeria el gazē'ir

Algerian (man, adjective) gaze'eeree; (woman) gaze'eeraya

Algiers el gazē'ir

alive *a-Iyish; **is he still alive?** hoowa lessa *a-Iyish?

all kul; **all the hotels** kul el fanādi'; **all my friends** kul asHaabee; **all my money** kul floosee; **all of it** kuloo; **all of them** kuloohum; **all right** kuloo tamam; **I'm all right** ana kwIyis; **that's all** bas kedda; **it's all changed** kuloo etghIyar; **thank you — not at all** shukran — el *afw

Allah allah; **praise be to Allah** el Hamdu lillah

allergic: I'm allergic to ... ana Hassas lil ...

allergy Hassasaya

alligator timseH

all-inclusive kuloo maHsoob fee

allowed masmōH; **is it allowed?** da masmōH?; **I'm not allowed to eat salt** ana mamnoo-a* min akl el malH

all-risks (insurance) kul el akhtaar

almost ta'reeban

alone waHeed; **are you alone?** inta li waHdak?; **leave me alone** sibnee li waHdee

already min abl

also kamen

alteration ta*deel

alternative: is there an alternative? fee badeel?; **we had no alternative** makensh *andenna badeel

alternator mō-walid kaharaabee

although bilraaghm min

altogether kuloohum; **what does that come to altogether?** kuloohum bikam?

always dIman

a.m.: at 8 a.m. e-sa*a tamania e-subH

amazing modhish

ambassador safeer

ambulance is*af; **get an ambulance** otlub el is*af

America amreeka

American (adjective) amreekee; (man) amreekānee; (woman) amreekanaya; **the Americans** el amreekan

American plan ikaama kamla

amoebic dysentery dusunteree-a, 'amoeba'

among bayn

an(a)esthetic beng

ancestors gedood

anchor helb

anchovies anshooga

ancient adeem

and wa

angina dee' nafas

angry za*lēn; **I'm very angry about it** ana za*lēn awee

animal HIawan

ankh ank

ankle asabit e-rigl (f)

anniversary *Iyeed; **it's our (wedding) anniversary today** *Iyeed zawagna e-sanawee e-naharda

annoy: he's annoying me hoowa midaye'nee; **it's so annoying** dee Haga tidayi'

another: can we have another room? mumkin ōda tania?; **another bottle, please** ezaza tania lowsamaHt

answer: there was no answer makensh fee ruhd; **what was his answer?** radoo kan ay?

ant: ants naml

antibiotics bensileen

antihistamine 'allergex' (*tm*)
antique: is it an antique? da anteek?
antique shop maHal anteeka
antiquities asaar
antisocial: don't be antisocial mateb'ash baykh
any: have you got any bread/milk? *andak *ı-esh/laban?; I haven't got any ma*andeesh
anybody: can anybody help me? mumkin Had yisa*ıdnee?; there wasn't anybody there makensh fee Had hinak
anything aya Haga; I don't want anything mush *a-ıyiz Haga; don't you have anything else? *andak Haga tania?
apart from monfassil
apartment sha'a
aperitif mashroobaat li fatH e-shahaya
apology e*atizaar; please accept my apologies e'bel e*atizaree lowsamaHt
appalling mor*ayb
appear: it would appear that ... min el waadeH en ...
appendicitis el a*war
appetite shahaya; I've lost my appetite maleesh nifs
apple tufaHa
application form taluhb ta'deem
appointment ma*ad; I'd like to make an appointment *a-ıyiz aHgiz ma*ad
appreciate: thank you, I appreciate it shukran giddan giddan
approve: she doesn't approve haya mush moo-waf'a
apricot mishmisha
April abreel
aqualung gehaz tanafuhs
Arab (*man, adjective*) *arabee; (*woman*) *arabaya; the Arabs el *arab
Arabic (*adjective*) *arabee; (*language*) lögha *arabaya
Arab League el gam*a el *arabaya
arch(a)eology asaar
are *see page 113*
area: I don't know the area ana mush *arif el monti'a

area code nimrit el monti'a
arm dira*
around *see* about
arrangement: will you make the arrangements? mumkin te*amil el lēzim?
arrest abuhd *ala; he's been arrested hoowa it'abuhd *alay
arrival wisool
arrive: when do we arrive? Hanewsuhl emta?; has my parcel arrived yet? e-tard bita*ee wasuhl?; let me know as soon as they arrive ollee awil mıyoosuhl; we only arrived yesterday eHna wasuhlna imbarraH bas
art fan
art gallery saalit *ard el finoon
arthritis eltihab el mafassil
artichoke kharshoofa
artificial (*man-made*) istin*ı; (*false*) moozayif
artist fanān
as: as fast as you can biasra* mıyumkin; as much as you can *ala ad mati'dar; as you like *ala kayfak; as it's getting late le'en el wa't mit'akhuhr
ashore lil shuht
ashtray tuhfıya
aside from monfassil
ask taluhb; that's not what I asked for ana mataluhbtish da; could you ask him to phone me back? mumkin ti'olloo yitessil baya?
asleep: he's still asleep hoowa lessa nayim
aspirin asbreen
assault: she's been assaulted it-hagam *alayha; indecent assault hegoom faadeH
assistant (*helper*) moosayıd; (*in shop*) (*male*) baya*; (*female*) baya*a
assume: I assume that ... ana azon en ...
asthma azma
astonishing modhish
Aswan aswaan
at: at the café *and el ahwa; at the

hotel *and el fondō'; **at 8 o'clock** e-sa*a tamania; **see you at dinner** ashoofak fil *asha
Atlantic Ocean el moнeed el atlantee
Atlas Mountains gibal uнtluhs
atmosphere (*weather*) e-gow
attractive нelw; **you're very attractive** (*to a woman*) intee нelwa awee
aubergine bitingaana
auction mazad *alanee
audience guhmhoor
August aghostos
aunt (*mother's sister*) khēlla; (*father's sister*) *amma
Australia ostralya
Australian (*man, adjective*) osturaalee; (*woman*) osturalaya
Austria e-nimsa
authorities e-sultaat
automatic ōtoomateekee

automobile *arabaya
autumn khareef; **in the autumn** fil khareef
available: when will it be available? emta нikoon gēhiz?; **when will he be available?** emta нikoon faadee?
avenue taree' mashuhguhr
average: the average Egyptian el masree el *adee; **an above average hotel** fondō' fō' el mōtawassit; **a below average hotel** fondō' taнt el mōtawassit; **the food was only average** el akl kan ma*ool; **on average** bimoo*adil
awake: is she awake? haya saнaya?
away: is it far away? da ba*yeed?; **go away!** imshee!
awful fazee-a*
axle (*front*) meнwar amāmee; (*rear*) meнwar khalfee

B

baby noonoo, 'baby'
baby-carrier 'carrycot'
baby-sitter dada; **can you get us a baby-sitter?** mumkin tegeeb lenna dada?
bachelor *azib
back (*of body*) dahr; **I've got a bad back** dahree mush kwıyis; **at the back** fil akher; **I'll be right back** нarga* *alatool; **when do you want it back?** *a-ızhoo emta?; **can I have my money back?** mumkin ekhud floosee?; **come back!** erga*!; **I go back home tomorrow** ana merowaн bukra; **we'll be back next year** нanerga*a e-sana e-gaya; **when is the last bus back?** emta akher ōtōbees?
backache: I have a backache *andee waga* fi dahree

back door bab waraanee
backgammon towla
backpack shanta li dahr
back seat korsee akher
bad: you are bad inta mo'zee; **this meat's bad** el laнma dee fazda; **a bad headache** suda* shedeed; **it's not bad** ma*ool; **too bad!** waнesh awee
badly: he's been badly injured e-sabtoo radee'a
bag (*suitcase*) shanta; (*carrier bag*) kees
baggage shōnuht
baggage allowance wazna magēnee
baggage checkroom maktab el amanēt
Bahrain el baнrayn
bakery foruhn
balcony (*in cinema*) balakōn; (*of house*) balakōna; **a room with a balcony**

oda bee balakōna; **on the balcony** fil balakōna

bald a'ra*

ball kora

ballet 'ballet'

ball-point pen alam gaf

banana mooza

band (*music*) fer'a

bandage roobaat shesh; **could you change the bandage?** mumkin tighayar roobaat e-shesh?

bandaid shireet laza'

bank bank; **when is the bank open?** el bank beeyeftaн emta?

bank account нisaab fil bank

bar 'bar'; **let's meet in the bar** mumkin nit'aabil fil 'bar'; **a bar of chocolate** shokalaata

barbecued meats laнma meshwaya

barber salōn нila'a

bargain: it's a real bargain dee lo'ta нa'ee-ee

barman garsōn

barrette bensa; (*with fancy decoration*) tooka

bartender garsōn

basic assassee; **the hotel is rather basic** el fondō' *adee khalis; **will you teach me some basic phrases?** mumkin te*alimnee ba*d e-gomal el assasaya?

basket (*storage*) afuhs; (*for shopping*) saabat

bath banyō; **can I take a bath?** mumkin asta*mil el banyō; **could you give me a bath towel?** mumkin teddeenee footit el нammem?

bathing costume mayoo

bathrobe rōb нammem

bathroom нammem; **a room with a private bathroom** ōda bi нammem; **can I use your bathroom?** mumkin e-tawalet, lowsamaнt?

battery battaraya; **the battery's flat** el battaraya fadia

bay khaleeg

bazaar soo'

be: be reasonable kheleek ma*ool; **don't be lazy** mateb'ash kaslān;

where have you been? (*to a man*) kunt fayn?; (*to a woman*) kuntee fayn?; **I've never been to Luxor** ana *omree maroнt lu'suhr; *see page 113*

beach bilasн; **on the beach** *alel bilasн; **I'm going to the beach** ana rтaн lil bilasн

beach mat нaseerit bilasн

beach towel footit bilasн

beach umbrella shamsayit bilasн

beads kharaz

beans (*green*) fasōlya; (*dried*) lobya; (*brown, dried*) fool

beard da'n (*f*)

beautiful gameel; **thank you, that's beautiful** shukran da нelwa awee

beauty salon salōn tagmeel

because *alashen; **because of the weather** bisabab e-gow

bed sireer; **single bed** sireer; **twin beds** sireerayn; **double bed** sireer litneen; **you haven't made my bed** ma*amalteesh sireeree; **he's still in bed** hoowa lessa fi sireer; **I'm going to bed** ana dekhil anam

bed and breakfast noom wiftar

bed linen bтyadaat

bedroom ōt e-noom

Beduin badawee; **the Beduin** badoo

bee naнla

beef fillay

beer beera; **two beers, please** ezaztayn beera, lowsamaнt

before abl; **before breakfast** abl el fetar; **before I leave** abl mamshee; **I haven't been here before** ana *omree magayt hena

beggar shaнat

begin: when does it begin? bitebda' emta?

beginner mobtadi'; **I'm just a beginner** ana lessa mobtadi'

beginning: at the beginning fil beedaya

behavio(u)r tasaruf

behind wara; **the driver behind me** e-saweh' ellee warтya

beige baysн

Beirut 'Beirut'

believe: I don't believe you ana mush misada'ak; **I believe you** ana misada'ak

bell guhras

belly-dance ra's shar'ee

bellydancer ra'aasa

belly-dancing ra's shar'ee

belong: that belongs to me da bita*ee; **who does this belong to?** da bita*a meen?

belongings: all my belongings kuloo mumtalakaatee

below taнt; **below the knee** taнt e-rukba; **below 50** a'al min khamseen

belt (*clothing*) нezam

bend (*in road*) malaf

berth (*on ship*) sireer

beside gamb; **beside the mosque** gamb e-gāmi*a; **sit beside me** o*ad gambee

besides: besides that kamen

best aнsen; **the best hotel in town** aнsen fondō' fil muhnti'a; **that's the best meal I've ever had** dee aнsen akla kalteha

bet rahan; **I bet you 50 piastres** arahnak khamseen uhrsh

better aнsen; **that's better!** kedda aнsen; **are you feeling better?** inta кwιyis?; **I'm feeling a lot better now** ana aнsen delwa'tee; **I'd better be going now** ana lezim amshee delwa'tee

between bayn

beyond ab*ad min; **beyond the desert** ab*ad min e-saнara

bicycle *agala; **can we rent bicycles here?** mumkin ni'guhr *agal hena?

big kebeer; **a big one** kebeer; **that's too big** da kebeer awee; **it's not big enough** (*too short*) osıyar awee; (*too small*) sooghıyar awee; (*not enough*) mush kifaya

bigger akbar; **do you have a bigger one?** *andak aya нaga akbar?

bike *agala

bikini bikeenee

bilharzia bilharissya

bill fatoora; **could I have the bill,**

please? mumkin el fatoora, lowsamaнt?

billfold maнfaza

billiards bileeyardō

birds teeyor

biro (*tm*) alam gaf

birthday *ıyeed milad; **it's my birthday** *ıyeed miladee; **when is your birthday?** *ıyeed miladuhk emta?; **happy birthday!** *ıyeed milad sa*yeed!

biscuit baskaweet

bit нetta; **just a little bit for me** нetta sooghıyara; **a big bit** нetta kebeera; **a bit of that cake** нetta min el kayk da; **it's a bit too big for me** (*in size*) da kebeer awee; (*in quantity*) da keteer awee; **it's a bit cold today** e-naharda bard shwıya

bite (*by insect*) uhrsa; (*by animal*) *ada; **I've been bitten** (*by insect*) ana et'aruhst; (*by dog*) kalb *adinee; **do you have something for insect bites?** *andak нaga li ars el нasharaat?

bitter (*taste*) morr

bitter lemon lamoon morr

black eswid; **black and white film** film abee-ad wi eswid

blackout: he's had a blackout hoowa oghma *alay

bladder mathuhna; (*colloquial word*) massuhna

blanket batanaya; **I'd like another blanket, please** batanaya tania lowsamaнt

blazer bilayzar

bleach (*for toilet etc*) bitahs

bleed: he's bleeding damoo sayyeн

bless you! (*after sneeze*) *anoo!

blind a*ama

blinds sattayar

blister kees mıya

blocked (*road, drain*) mazdood

block of flats *omara

blond (*hair*) asfuhr; (*colouring*) ash'ar

blonde (*noun*) sha'ra

blood dam; **his blood group is ...** damoo magmoo*a ...; **I have high**

blood pressure *andee erteefa*a fi
daght e-dam
blouse bilooza
blue azra'
blusher (*cosmetic*) bankeek
board: full board ikaama kamla;
half-board nus ikaama
boarding house benseeyōn
boarding pass bita'it so*ood
boat markib; **Egyptian sailing boat**
felooka
body gisma
boil (*on body*) dimil; **boil the water**
eghlee el mıya
boiled egg bayda masloo'a
boiling hot (*weather, food*) sukhn narr
bomb (*noun*) kombilla
bone (*in meat, body*) *adma; (*in fish*)
shōka
bonnet (*of car*) kaboot
book (*noun*) kitab; **I'd like to book a
table for two** mumkin aнgiz
tarabayza litneen
bookshop, bookstore maktaba
boot (*on foot*) boot; (*of car*) shanta
booze koнol; **I had too much booze**
ana shribt keteer
border (*of country*) нedood
bored: I'm bored ana zeh'en
boring mumil
born: I was born in ... (*date/place*) ana
etwalat fi ...
borrow: may I borrow ...? mumkin
estayeer; (*money*) mumkin estelif ...?
boss rıyis
both: I'll take both of them наkhud
litneen; **we'll both come** eнna
litneen наneegee
bother: sorry to bother you asif *alel
iz*ag; **it's no bother** mush mōhim;
it's such a bother da kuloo mata*ıb
bottle ezaza; **a bottle of wine** ezazit
nebeez; **another bottle, please** ezaza
tania lowsamaнt
bottle-opener fatēнa
bottom (*base*) a*ada; **at the bottom of
the Pyramids** *and a*dit el нaram
bottom gear elowel
bouncer (*at club*) fitowaa (*m*)

bowels masareen
box sandoo'
box office shebek tazēkir
boy walad
boyfriend: my boyfriend saнibee
bra sinteeyen
bracelet iswera
brake fluid zayt faraamil
brake lining bitaanit el faraamil
brakes faraamil; **there's something
wrong with the brakes** fee *ıyib fil
faraamil; **can you check the brakes?**
mumkin tekshif *alel faraamil?; **I
had to brake suddenly** edtarayt
afaarmil bisora*a
brandy 'cognac'
brass naнas asfar; **made of brass** min
e-naнas
brave shuga*
bread *ı-esh; **could we have some
bread and butter?** mumkin *ı-esh
wee zebda?; **some more bread,
please** *ı-esh tanee, lowsamaнt;
white bread feenō; **wholemeal bread**
*ı-esh baladee; **white pitta bread** *ı-
esh shāmee
break kuнsuhr; **I think I've broken
my ankle** azon inee kuнsuhrt asabit
riglee; **it keeps breaking** dıman
titkuнsuhr
breakdown: I've had a breakdown
(*in a car*) *arabeetee et*atalit;
nervous breakdown inheeyar
*asabee
breakfast fetar; **English breakfast**
fetar ingileezee; **full breakfast** fetar
kaamil; **continental breakfast** fetar
'continental'
break in: somebody's broken in
наraamee dakhel hena
breast (*chest*) sedr; (*woman's breast*) bez
breast-feed reeda*a
breath nafas; **out of breath** mafeesh
nafas
breathe: I can't breathe mush adir
atnafis
breathtaking museer
breeze nisma
bridal suite ginaн el *arsen

bride *aroosa
bridegroom *arees
bridge (*over river*) kubree
brief (*stay, visit*) mokhtassir
briefly bekhtisaar
briefcase shanta
bright (*colour*) zaahee; **bright red** aнmar zaahee
brilliant (*idea*) momtaz; (*colour*) moowahwig
bring gab; **could you bring it to my hotel?** mumkin tegeeboo lil fondō' bita*ee?; **I'll bring it back** ana нaraga*oo; **can I bring a friend too?** mumkin ageeb saнbee ma*aya?
Britain ingilterra
British ingileezee; **the British** el ingileez
brochure matboo-*a; **do you have any brochures on ...?** *andak matboo-*aat *an ...?
broke: I'm broke ana mifalis
broken maksoor; **you've broken it** inta kasartoo; **it's broken** maksoor; **broken nose** anf maksoor
brooch brōsн
brother akh; **my brother** akhooya
brother-in-law: my brother-in-law (*wife's brother*) akhoo miraatee; (*husband's brother*) akhoo goozee
brown bonee; **I don't go brown** ana mabasmarsh
browse: may I just browse around? mumkin atfarag?
bruise (*noun*) waram azra'
brunette bonee
brush (*noun*) forsha
bucket gardel
buffalo gamoosa
buffet 'buffet'
bug (*insect*) нashara; **bed bugs** ba'; **she's caught a bug** *andaha a*adwa
building mabna
bulb (*electrical*) luнnda; **a new bulb** luнnda gedeeda
bull *a-ıgl
bullfrog dovda*a
bulrushes nabat el baardee
bump khabt; **I bumped my head** khabat raasee
bumper ekseedaam
bumpy (*road, flight*) matabaat
bunch of flowers bookay ward
bungalow bayt ardee
bunion tawalwul fi rigl
bunk beds sireer bidoorayn
buoy *awaama
burglar наrámee
burn нar'; **do you have an ointment for burns?** *andak maraham lil нuroo'?
burnt манroo'; **this meat is burnt** el laнma dee манuroo'a; **my arms are so burnt** diroo*ı манuroo'a awee
burst: a burst pipe masoora mifar'a*a
bus ōtōbees; **is this the bus for ...?** el ōtōbees da rıyaн ...?; **when's the next bus?** (*while at stop*) el ōtōbees gay emta?; (*when booking*) emta el ōtōbees ellee ba*dō?
bus driver sawē' ōtōbees
business shoghl; **I'm here on business** ana hena fi shoghl; **it's a pleasure to do business with you** yisharuhfnee el *amil ma*a seeyatak
bus station mow'af ōtōbees
bus stop маHatit ōtōbees; **will you tell me which bus stop I get off at?** mumkin ti'ollee anzil fayn?
bust (*of body*) sedr
bus tour gowla mōnazuhma
busy (*street, restaurant*) masнghool; **I'm busy this evening** ana masнghool elleelādee; **the line was busy** (*telephone*) el khad kan masнghool
but laakin; **not ... but ...** mush ... laakin ...
butcher guhzar
butter zebda
butterfly faraasha
button zoorar
buy: I'll buy it нashteree; **where can I buy ...?** fayn ashteree ...?
by bil; **by boat** bil markib; **by car** bil *arabaya; **by train** bil atr; **who's it written by?** meen kataboo?; **I came by myself** gayt lee waнdee; **a seat**

by the window korsee gamb e-
shebek; **by the sea** gamb el baнr;
can you do it by Wednesday?

mumkin te*amiloo *ala yum el
arba*?
bye-bye 'bye-bye'

C

cab (*taxi*) taksee; (*fixed price from airport*) limōzeen
cabaret 'cabaret'
cabbage kuromba
cabin kabeena
cable (*electrical*) silk kaharaba
café ahwa
caffeine 'caffeine'
Cairo el kaheera
cake kayk; **a piece of cake** нettit kayk
calculator 'calculator'
calendar nateega
caliph khaleefa (*m*); **tombs of the
caliphs** ma'aabir el khaleefa
call: what is this called? da ismoo
ay?; **call the manager!** inda el
modeer!; **I'd like to make a call to
England** ana *a-ıyiz a*mil mokalma
lingilterra; **I'll call back later** (*come
back*) нarga* tanee; (*phone back*)
нatessil tanee; **I'm expecting a call
from London** ana mestannee
mokalma min 'london'; **would you
give me a call at 7.30?** mumkin
tetessil baya e-sa*a saba*a wi nus?;
it's been called off itlagha
call box telefōn
calm (*person, sea*) hedee; **calm down!**
ehedda!
Calor gas (*tm*) uhnboobit bootagaz
calories waнedaat нarraraya
camel gamal
camel driver ra*ee e-gimāl
camel racing sibe' e-gimāl
**camel ride: how much is a camel
ride to the sphinx?** bikam lee aboo
el нōl?; **I'd like to ride a camel —
how much is it?** ana *a-ıyiz arkab

gamal — bikam?
camel train kaafillit gimāl
camera 'camera'
**camp: is there somewhere we can
camp?** fee makken mumkin
nay*askuhr fee?; **can we camp here?**
mumkin nay*askuhr hena?
campbed sireer khayma
camping takheem
campsite ma*askuhr shebeb
can (*tin*) safeeнa; **a can of mango
juice** *albit manga
can: can I ...? mumkin ana ...?; **can
you ...?** mumkin inta ...?; **can he ...?**
mumkin hoowa ...?; **can she ...?**
mumkin haya ...?; **can we ...?**
mumkin eнna ...?; **can they ...?**
mumkin humma ...?; **I can't ...**
ma'adarsh ...; **he can't ...** hoowa
mayi'darsh ...; **can I keep it?**
mumkin aнtuhfiz bee?; **if I can**
lowa'dar; **that can't be right** da
ghalat
Canada 'canada'
Canadian (*man, adjective*) kanadee;
(*woman*) kanadaya
cancel lagha; **can I cancel my
reservation?** mumkin elghee el
нagz bita*ee?; **can we cancel dinner
for tonight?** mumkin nilghee el
*asha elleelādee?; **I cancelled it**
ana laghaytoo
cancellation ghe'
candle sham*a
candies (*in wrappers*) bon bon; (*general
term for sweets*) нalawee-at; **a piece of
candy** нettit нalawee-at
can-opener fataнa

cap ghuhtaa; **bathing cap** bonnay lil sibaHa

capital city el medeena e-ra'eesaya

capital letters Haroof kebeera

capsize: it capsized it'alabit

captain (of ship) 'captain'

car *arabaya

carafe 'carafe'

carat: is it 9/14 carat gold? da *ayar tis*a/arba*ataashar?

caravan (of camels) kaafilla

carbonated fawarr

carburet(t)or kaarbrete-ir

card: do you have a (business) card? ma*ak kart?

cardboard box *alba kartōn

cardigan bullōvar maftooHa

cards kutsheena; **do you play cards?** bitil*ab kutsheena?

care: goodbye, take care ma*a salemma, khelee baalak min nafsak; **will you take care of this bag for me?** mumkin tekhud baalak min e-shanta dee?; **care of ...** bitaruhf ...

careful: be careful! khelee baalak!

careless: that was careless of you da ehmal minak; **careless driving** seewaa' bi ehmal

car ferry ma*adaya

car hire ta'geer *arabeeyaat

car keys mufatiyaH el *arabaya

carnation oronfil

carnival 'carnival'

car park mow'af *arabeeyaat

carpet sigada

car rental (place) maktab ta'geer *arabeeyaat

carriage (with horse) Hantoor

carrots guhzuhr

carry shel; **could you carry this for me?** mumkin tisheel da *alashēnee?

carry-all shanta

carry-cot 'carrycot'

car-sick: I get car-sick ana *andee dawakhen safar

Carthage kortaag

carton kartōn; **a carton of milk** kartōnet laban

carving naHt

carwash gheseel *arabaya

Casablanca e-daar el bIdaa'

case (suitcase) shanta; **in any case** fee ay Hala; **in that case** fil Hala dee; **it's a special case** dee Hala khasa; **in case he comes back** fee Haalet reegoo*a tanee; **I'll take two just in case** Hakhud itneen lil Huhrs

cash feloos; **I don't have any cash** ma*eesh feloos; **I'll pay cash** Hatfa*kesh; **will you cash a cheque/check for me?** mumkin tesriflee sheek?

cashdesk (in shop) kays

cash dispenser el bank e-shakhsee

cash register khazna

casino 'casino'

cassette 'cassette'

cassette player, cassette recorder tazgeel

castle asr

casual: casual clothes malābis shebab

cat ota

catacombs saradeeb

catamaran 'catamaran'

catastrophe museeba

catch: where do we catch the bus? minayn nakhud el ōtōbees?; **he's caught some strange illness** hoowa *andoo marad ghereeb mo*adee

catching: is it catching? da mo*adee?

cathedral kattedra-aya

Catholic (adjective) kathlik

cauliflower aranabeet

cause sabab

cave maghara

caviar koviar

ceiling sa'f

celebrations eHtifel

cellophane suloofen

cemetery madfen; (historic, Islamic) ma'aabir

center west; see also **centre**

centigrade ma'awaya; see page 119

centimetre, centimeter 'centimetre'; see page 117

central ra'eesee; **we'd prefer something more central** eHna nifaduhl Haga fee west el balad

central station el maнatta e-ra'eesaya

centre west; **how do we get to the centre?** izay noosal li west el balad?; **in the centre (of town)** fee west el balad

century meet sana; **in the 19th century** fil arn e-tisa*taashar; **in the 20th century** fil arn el *ashreen

ceramics khazaf

certain mutakid; **are you certain?** inta mutakid?; **I'm absolutely certain** ana mutakid awee

certainly tab*an; **certainly not** la' tab*an

certificate shaheda; **birth certificate** shahedit meelad

chain (for bike) ganzeer; (around neck) silsilla

chair korsee

chalet 'chalet'

chambermaid khadamit el ghorfa

champagne shambania

chance: quite by chance bi sodfa; **no chance!** mafeesh forsa!

change: could you change this into pounds? mumkin teghiyar da lee ginahat?; **I haven't got any change** ma*eesh faka; **can you give me change for a 10 pound note?** mumkin tifukilee *ashara ginay?; **do we have to change (trains)?** eнna lezim nighiyar?; **for a change** litagheer; **you haven't changed the sheets** intee maghiyarteesh; **the place has changed so much** el maken etghiyar khalis; **do you want to change places with me?** *a-iyiz teghiyar maken ma*ya?; **can I change this for ...?** mumkin aghiyar da lee ...?

changeable (weather) muta'alib

chaos hargalla

chap raagil; **the chap at reception** e-raagil *and el esta*lamat

charge: is there an extra charge? fee ay zeeyada?; **what do you charge?** bitakhud ad ay?; **who's in charge here?** meen e-riyis hena?

charming badee-a*

chart (diagram) rasma bayanee; (for navigation) khareeta baнaraya

charter flight reнla khasa

chassis 'chassis'

cheap rekhees; **do you have something cheaper?** *andak aya нaga arakhas?

cheat ghash; **I've been cheated** ana etghashayt

check: will you check? mumkin teragaa*?; **will you check the steering?** mumkin tekshif *ala e-drikseeōn; **will you check the bill?** mumkin teragaa* *alel fatoora; **I've checked it** ana regaa*taha

check (financial) sheek; **will you take a check?** bitekhud sheekat?

check (bill) fatoora; **may I have the check please?** mumkin el fatoora lowsamaнt?

checkbook duhftuhr sheekat

checked (shirt etc) muraba*at

checkers seega

check-in morag*ıt el kowntuhr

checkroom (for coats etc) amanēt

cheek (on face) khed; **what a cheek!** ya salām!

cheeky (person) bigaн

cheerio (bye-bye) 'bye-bye'

cheers (thank you) shukran; (toast) fee seнetuhk

cheer up farfish kedda

cheese gibna

chef 'chef'

chemist (shop) agzakhenna

cheque sheek; **will you take a cheque?** bitekhud sheekat?

cheque book duhftuhr sheekat

cherry kerez

chess shataruhng

chest (body) sedr

chewing gum leban

chicken ferēkh

chickenpox el gōdaree

child tefl

child minder dāda

child minding service нadaana

children atfaal

children's playground mal*ab lil

atfaal

children's pool Hammem sibaHa lil
atfaal

chilled (*wine*) sa'a*; **it's not properly
chilled** da mush sa'a*

chilly bard

chimney madkhana

chin da'uhn (*f*)

china seenee

chips bataatis maHamara (*f*); **potato
chips** chips

chocolate shokalaata; **a chocolate bar**
shokalaata; **a box of chocolates**
*albit shokalaata; **a hot chocolate**
kakow

choke (*on car*) howa

cholera 'cholera'

choose ekhtar; **it's hard to choose**
min esa*ab tekhtar; **you choose for
us** inta tekhtar *alashēnna

chop: a lamb chop reesha dahnee

Christian (*noun, adjective*) miseeHee

Christian name ism

Christmas *Iyeed milad el messeeaH;
merry Christmas *Iyeed milad
sa*yeed

church kineesa; **where is the
Protestant church?** fayn el kineesa
el brotestaneea?; **where is the
Catholic church?** fayn el kineesa el
katholeekaya?

cigar sigar

cigarette sigara; **tipped cigarettes**
sigara bee filtar; **plain cigarettes**
sigara min gheer filtar

cigarette lighter walla*at saggayar

cine-camera kamera sinema'aya

cinema 'cinema'

circle Hala'a; (*in theatre*) balakōn

citadel al*a

citizen: I'm a British citizen ana
ingileezee; **I'm an American citizen**
ana amrikānee

city medeena

city centre, city center west el balad

claim (*noun: insurance*) ta*oweed

claim form talab ta*oweed

clarify wadaH

classical klassik

classical Arabic logha *arabaya

clean (*adjective*) nedeef; **it's not clean**
mush nedeef; **may I have some
clean sheets?** mumkin tedeenee
milayaat nedeefa?; **our apartment
hasn't been cleaned today** sha'a etna
matnadafetsh e-naharda; **can you
clean this for me?** mumkin
tenaduhf da *alashenee?

cleaning solution (*for contact lenses*)
maHlool lituhndeef

cleansing cream (*cosmetic*) 'cream'
lituhndeef

clear: it's not very clear da mush
waadeH; **ok, that's clear** ok da
waadeH

clever shaater

cliff hafit e-gabal

climate e-gow

climb: it's a long climb to the top
matla* taweel

clinic *Iyeda

cloakroom (*for coats*) amanēt; (*WC*)
tawalet

clock sa*at Hayta

close: is it close? da ora-Iyib?; **close
to the hotel** ora-Iyib min el fondō';
close by mush ba*yeed

close (*verb*) afel; **when do you close?**
bite'fil emta?

closed aafil; **they were closed** kan
aafil

closet (*cupboard*) dooleb

cloth (*material*) oomash; (*rag*) Hettit
oomash

clothes hedoom

clothes line Habl ghaseel

clothes peg, clothespin mashbak

clouds saHab

cloudy maghayim

club nēdee

clubs (*cards*) isbātee

clumsy a*ma

clutch (*car*) debree-aSH; **the clutch is
slipping** e-debree-aSH beeyeflet

coach (*long distance bus*) ōtōbees safar

coach party fōg

coach trip reHla seeyaHaya

coast saaHil el baHr; **at the coast** *and

saaHil el baнr
coastguard *amil inkaaz
coat (*overcoat etc*) baltoo; (*jacket*) sHakit
coathanger shama*a
cobbler gazmagee
cockroach sorsaar
cocktail 'cocktail'
cocktail bar 'cocktail bar'
cocoa kakow
coconut guz el hind
**code: what's the (dialling) code for
...?** rakuhm 'code' ... ay?
coffee ahwa; **a white coffee, a coffee
with milk** ahwa bee laban; **a black
coffee** ahwa sēda; **two coffees,
please** itneen ahwa lowsamaнt
coffee pot kanaka
coin *omla
Coke (*tm*) kakōla
cold (*adjective*) bard; **I'm cold** ana
bardēn; **I have a cold** ana *andee
zookam
cold cream (*cosmetic*) 'cream'
collapse: he's collapsed oghma *alay
collar ye'a
collar bone *admit e-tarwa'a
colleague saHib; **my colleague**
saHibee; **your colleague** saHbak
collect: I've come to collect ... ana
gayt akhud; **I collect ...** (*stamps etc*)
ana bagma* ...
collect call *this service is not yet possible
from Egypt*
college kullaya
collision tuhsadum
colloquial Egyptian Arabic lahga
muhsraya
cologne kulonia
colossus timsēl
colo(u)r lōn; **do you have any other
colo(u)rs?** *andak alwān tania?
colo(u)r film film milowin
column (*of temple etc*) *amood
comb (*noun*) misht
come gay; **I come from London** ana
gay min 'london'; **where do you
come from?** inta minayn?; **when are
they coming?** humma gayeen emta?;
come here ta*ala hena; **come with**

me ta*ala ma*ya; **come back!** erga*!;
I'll come back later ana harga*
tanee; **come in!** itfuhduhl!; **he's
coming on very well** (*improving*)
hoowa etHassin awee; **come on!**
yalla!; **do you want to come out this
evening?** *a-Iyiz tukhrug elleelādee?;
these two pictures didn't come out
esortayn dōl matel*a-owsh; **the
money hasn't come through yet** el
feloos lessa magetsh
comfortable (*hotel etc*) moreeH; **it's
not very comfortable** mush moreeH
Common Market e-soo' el orōbee
company (*firm*) shirka; **my company**
shirkitee
comparison shabeh; **there's no
comparison** maloosh maseel
compartment (*train*) saloon
compass bosla
compensation ta*weed
complain ishtaka; **I want to
complain about my room** *a-Iyiz
ashtikee *an otee
complaint shakwa; **I have a
complaint** *andee shakwa
complete kaamil; **the complete set**
ta'm kaamil; **it's a complete disaster**
museeba kebeera
completely tamaamem
complicated ma*a'd; **it's very
complicated** da ma*a'd awee
**compliment: my compliments to the
chef** taHayaatee li 'chef'
comprehensive (*insurance*) shaamil
compulsory darooree
computer 'computer'
concern: we are very concerned
eHna ala'neen awee
concert Hafla moosikaya
concussion ertigag
condenser (*in car*) 'condenser'
condition (*state*) Hala; **it's not in very
good condition** da mush fee Hala
kwIyissa khalis
conditioner (*for hair*) balsam
condom kaboot
conductor (*on train*) komsaree
conference mo'tammuhr

confirm akid; **can you confirm the reservation?** mumkin te-akid el Hagz?

confuse: it's very confusing da akhuhr rabka

congratulations! mabrook!

conjunctivitis eltihab eb multaHeema

connection (*in travelling*) wosla

connoisseur khabeer

conscious (*medically*) way*I-ee

consciousness: he's lost consciousness hoowa fakad wa*Iyoo

constipation imsek

consul 'consul'

consulate konsulaya

contact: how can I contact ...? izzay attessil bee ...?; **I'm trying to contact ...** ana beHowil attessil bee ...

contact lenses *adessēt laska

contraceptive (*noun*) mene*a lil Haml

contract (*noun*) *a'd

convenient (*time, location*) moola'im; **that's not convenient** da mush moola'im

cook: it's not properly cooked (*is underdone*) da nIyee; **it's beautifully cooked** da mistawee *Iz e-talab; **he's a good cook** hoowa tabakh kwIyis

cooker bootagaz

cookie baskaweet

cool (*day, weather*) mooratub

copper naHas aHmar

coppersmith naHas

copt obtee

coptic obtee

coral morgān

coral reef sho*ab morgānee

corduroy ateefa midulla*a

coriander kuzbarra

cork (*in bottle*) fil

corkscrew bareema lifataH el azayz

corn (*on foot*) kuhloo

corner: on the corner (*of street*) *alal nassia; **in the corner** fil rukn; **a corner table** tarabayza lil rukn

cornflakes 'cornflakes'

coronary (*noun*) zabHa suhdraya

correct (*adjective*) saH; **please correct me if I make a mistake** saHaHnee

lowsamaHt

corridor tor'a

corset korsay

cosmetics mawad tagmeel

cost: what does it cost? bikam?

cot (*for baby*) mahd; (*campbed*) sireer khayma

cottage bayt reefee

cotton oton

cotton buds (*for make-up removal etc*) otna tebee

cotton wool otna tebee

couch kanaba

cough (*noun*) кона

cough tablets bastilya

cough medicine dowa кона (*m*)

could: could you ...? mumkin ...?; **could I have ...?** mumkin ...?; **I couldn't ...** ma'adarsh ...

country (*nation*) wotuhn; **in the country** (*countryside*) fil reef

countryside reef

couple (*man and woman*) mitgowzeen; **a couple of boys** waladayn; **a couple of days** yōmayn; *see page 100*

courier morafik seeyaHee

course: of course bitaba*; **of course not** la' taba*an

court (*law*) maHkama; (*tennis*) mal*ab 'tennis'

courtesy bus (*airport to hotel etc*) ōtōbees magēnee

cousin: my cousin (*on mother's side*) (*aunt's daughter*) bint khaltee; (*aunt's son*) ibn khaltee; (*uncle's daughter*) bint khelee; (*uncle's son*) ibn khelee; (*on father's side*) (*aunt's daughter*) bint *amitee; (*aunt's son*) ibn *amitee; (*uncle's daughter*) bint *amee; (*uncle's son*) ibn *amee

cow ba'ra

crab kaaboree-a

cracked: it's cracked (*plate etc*) da mishrookh

cracker (*biscuit*) baskaweet

craftshop maHal maharaat yadawaya

cramp (*in leg etc*) shed *adalee

crankshaft krank

crash Hadsa; **there's been a crash** kan

fee Hadsa

crash course (*for learning language etc*) kors mokassif

crash helmet khooza

crawl (*swimming*) krol

crazy mahfoof

cream (*on milk, in cake, for face*) 'cream'

creche (*for babies*) Hadaana

credit card 'credit card'

crib (*baby's cot*) mahd

crisis azma

crisps 'chips'

crockery fokhar

crocodile timseH

crook: he's a crook hoowa nassaab

crossing (*by sea*) *aboor

crossroads takaata* toro'

crosswalk *aboor el mooshaa

crowd nas keteer; (*at football match etc*) mootafaregeen

crowded (*streets, bars*) zaHma

crown (*on tooth*) tag

crucial: it's absolutely crucial darooree giddan giddan

cruise: a cruise down the Nile reHla neelaya

crutches *owkez

cry (*weep*) baka; **don't cry** matebkeesh

cucumber (*small*) kheeyar; (*big*) at-ta

cuisine tuhbkh

cultural sakaafee

cummin kamoon

cup fingal; **a cup of coffee** fingal aHwa

cupboard doolab

cure: have you got something to cure it? *andak Haga te*aleghoo?

curlers roolee

current (*electrical*) tIyar kaharabee; (*in water*) tIyar

curry boohar hindee

curtains settayar

curve (*noun: in road*) malaf

cushion makhada

custom gomruk

Customs gamarek

cut: I've cut myself ana *owart nafsee; **could you cut a little off here?** mumkin te'ta* Hetta min hena?; **we were cut off** (*telephone*) el khat et'ata*; **the engine keeps cutting out** el mator bee'ata*

cutlery fuhdeeyaat

cutlets reesh

cycle: can we cycle there? (*is it far?*) mumkin nerooHa bil *agal?

cylinder (*of car*) 'cylinder'

cylinder-head gasket sHeewān

cynical mustahzi'

Cyprus kobros

cystitis eltihab fil masaana

D

dam sad

damage khoosara; **you've damaged it** inta khasartoo; **it's damaged** khasrit; **there's no damage** mafeesh khoosara

damn! ela*na!

damp (*adjective*) minadee

dance: a local traditional dance ra's sha*bee; **belly-dance** ra's shar'ee; **do you want to dance?** (*to a woman*) *a- Iza tur'ussee?

dancer: he's a good dancer hoowa ra'as Helw

dancing ra's; **we'd like to go dancing** *Izeen nerooH nur'us; **traditional Egyptian dancing** ra's baladee

dandruff eshr

dangerous khatar

dare: I don't dare ana ma*andeesh elgara'a

dark (*adjective*) duhlma; **dark blue** azra' ghēmi'; **when does it get dark?** bitduhlim emta?; **after dark** bil layl

darling Habeebee

dashboard tablō el *arabaya

date: what's the date? e-tareekh ay?; **on what date?** fee tareekh ay?; **can we make a date?** (*romantic, to business partner*) mumkin niratib ma*ad?

dates (*to eat*) balaH

daughter bint; **my daughter** bintee

daughter-in-law miratibnee

dawn (*noun*) fagr; **at dawn** fil fagr

day yum; **the day after** el yum ellee ba*do; **the day before** el yum ellee ablō; **every day** kul yum; **one day** fee yum min el ayem; **can we pay by the day?** mumkin nedfa* bil yōmaya?; **have a good day!** yum sa*yeed!

daylight robbery (*extortionate prices*) ser'a fee *ız e-nahar

day trip reHla yōmaya

dead mayit

deaf atruhsh

deaf-aid sama*a

deal (*business*) suhfuhka; **it's a deal** itafa'na; **will you deal with it?** mumkin ti-oom bee?

dealer (*agent*) taagir

dear (*expensive*) ghelee; **Dear Sir** e-sayid el *azzeez; **Dear Madam** e-sayida el *azzeeza; **Dear Adel** *azzeezee *adel

death mōt

decadent fee tadahworr

December disimbuhr

decent: that's very decent of you da akher zō' minak

decide suhmim; **we haven't decided yet** lessa massuhmimnash; **you decide for us** inta tesuhmim; **it's all decided** kuloo itsuhmim

decision karar

deck (*on ship*) zahr e-safeena

deckchair korsee lil bilaSH

declare: I have nothing to declare ma*aya fee Hedood el masmooH

decoration (*in room*) dicor

deduct khasm

deep ghaweet; **is it deep?** da ghaweet?

deep-freeze (*noun*) frayzuhr

definitely tab*an; **definitely not** la' tab*an

degree (*university*) shehada gami*ıya; (*temperature*) daraga

dehydrated (*person*) mayit min el *atuhsh; (*medically*) mōgafuhf

delay: the flight was delayed ma*ad e-tıyara etakher

deliberately biluhsd

delicacy: a local delicacy akl maHallee

delicious lazeez

deliver wasal; **will you deliver it?** mumkin tewasaloo?

delivery: is there another mail delivery? fee towzee*-a bareed tanee?

delta deltuh

de luxe luks

denims sHeenz

dent: there's a dent in it fee khabta

dentist garaH asnan

dentures ta'm asnan

deny: he denies it hoowa beeyenkir

deodorant moozeel lireeHet el *ara'

department store maHal kebeer

departure suhfar

departure lounge saalit e-suhfar

depend: it depends yimkin; **it depends on ...** ya-a*timid *ala ...

deposit (*noun: downpayment*) rahan

depressed Hazeen

depth *omk

dervish darweesh

description wasf

desert saHara; **in the desert** fi saHara

deserted (*beach, area*) mahgoor

dessert Helw

destination: what's your destination? rıaH fayn?

detergent monozif

detour taHweela

devalued alit imtoo

develop Hamuhd; **could you develop these films?** mumkin teHamuhd el

aflam dee?
diabetic (*noun*) muhreed bee sukar
diagram rasm bayānee
dialect laḥaga maḥalaya
dialling code nimra, 'code'
diamond maas
diamonds (*cards*) deenēree
diaper kafoola
diarrhoea, diarrhea is-hal; **do you have something to stop diarrhoea?** *andak Ḥaga lil is-hal?
diary moofakera
dictionary kaamoos; **an English/ Arabic dictionary** kaamoos ingileezee/*arabee
didn't *see* not *and page 112*
die mat; **I'm absolutely dying for a drink** ana mayit min el *atuhsh
diesel (*fuel*) 'diesel'
diet resḤeem; **I'm on a diet** ana ba*mil resḤeem
difference fer'a; **what's the difference between ...?** ay el fer'a bayn ...?; **I can't tell the difference** mush a'dar afer'a binhoom; **it doesn't make any difference** ma*alesh
different mokhtalif; **they are different** dōl mokhtalifeen; **they are very different** dōl mokhtalifeen awee; **it's different from this one** da mokhtalif *and da; **may we have a different table?** mumkin negḥıyar e-tarabayza?; **ah well, that's different** ah, da mokhtalif
difficult sa*b
difficulty sa*ōba; **without any difficulty** min gheer ay sa*ōba; **I'm having difficulties with ...** ana *andee mashēkil ma* ...
digestion haaduhm
dinghy markib sooghıyar
dining car 'buffet'
dining room (*at home*) ōdit suhfra; (*in hotel*) saalit el akl
dinner *asha
dinner jacket sḤakit smōkin
dinner party Ḥaflit *asha
dipped headlights e-noor el *adee
dipstick me'yes zayt

direct (*adjective*) mōbēshir; **does it go direct?** bayrooḤ mōbēshir?
direction etigah; **in which direction is it?** fee ay etigah?; **is it in this direction?** fil e-tigaḤ da?
directory: telephone directory daleel e-telefonēt
directory enquiries daleel telefonēt
dirt wosekha
dirty mush nedeef
disabled *agiz
disagree: it disagrees with me (*food*) mabit wafi'neesh
disappear ekhtafaa; **it's just disappeared** ekhtafet
disappointed: I was disappointed ana kheb amalee
disappointing: disappointing news akhbar tiza*al; **it was disappointing** kan yiza*al
disaster karsa
discharge (*pus*) khaalees
disc jockey 'disc jockey'
disco 'disco'
disco dancing ra's gharbee
discount (*noun*) takhfeed
disease marad
disgusting (*taste, food etc*) mu'rif
dish (*meal*) akla; (*plate*) tab'a
dishcloth foota
dishwashing liquid se'il lighasl e-saḤoon
disinfectant (*noun*) mootaher
disk of film 'disk'
dislocated shoulder kitf mafsool
dispensing chemist sıyeeduhlee
disposable nappies nabee, kafoola tusta*mal mara waḤda
distance masēfa; **what's the distance from ... to ...?** el masēfa aday min ... illa ...?; **in the distance** ba*yeed
distilled water mıya ma'atara
distributor (*in car*) asbritēr
disturb aza*ag; **the disco is disturbing us** e-disco za*agna
diversion (*traffic*) taḤweela
diving board manat
divorced metuhl'a
dizzy daykh; **I feel dizzy** ana daykh

dizzy spells dōkha
Djibouti sнuhbootee
do: what shall I do? a*mil ay?; **what are you doing tonight?** нata*mil ay elleelādee?; **how do you do it?** bita*miloo izzay?; **will you do it for me?** muмkin te*amiloo *alashēnee?; **who did it?** meen *amaloo?; **the meat's not done** el laнma dee nıya; **what do you do?** (job) bitishteghel ay?; **do you have ...?** *andak ...?
docks arsifet el meena
doctor doktor; **he needs a doctor** hoowa meнtag doktor; **can you call a doctor?** muмkin tutlub doktor?
document mustannad
dog kalb
doll *aroosa le*aba
dollar dollar
dome oba
donkey нomar
don't! la'; *see* **not** *and page 112*
door bab
doorman (for apartments etc) bewab; (for hotel) 'doorman'
dosage gura*a
double: double room ōda litneen; **double bed** sireer litneen; **double brandy** dobl brandee; **double r** (in spelling name) 'reh reh'; **it's all double Dutch to me** mish fēhim uhduhk
doubt: I doubt it maftikersh
douche (medical) нo'na
down: get down! enzil!; **he's not down yet** (is in room, bed) hoowa lessa manzelsh; **further down the road** odam shwıya; **I paid 20% down** ana defa*at *ashreen fil maya mō'adam
downmarket (restaurant, hotel) rekhees
downstairs e-dōr e-taнtānee
dozen dasta; **half a dozen** nus dasta
drain (noun: in sink, street) bala*a
draughts (game) seega
draughty: it's rather draughty el howa shedeed shwıya
drawing pin daboos rasm
dreadful (food, holiday, weather etc)

mush kwıyis
dream (noun) нelm; **it's like a bad dream** (this trip etc) zıyee kaboos; **sweet dreams** aнlam sa*yeeda
dress (woman's) foostan; **I'll just get dressed** нat-khul albis
dressing (for wound) gheeyar; (for salad) salsa
dressing gown rōb shambar
drink (verb) shirib; **can I get you a drink?** teshrab нaga?; **I don't drink** (alcohol) mabashrabsh; **I must have something to drink** (alcoholic and non-alcoholic) ana lezim ashrab нaga; **a long cool drink** mashroob sa'a*dobl; **may I have a drink of water?** muмkin kubayit mıya?; **drink up!** eshrab!; **I had too much to drink** ana shribt keteer
drinkable: is the water drinkable? el mıya salнa lil shorb?
drive seh'; **we drove here** gayna bil *arabaya; **I'll drive you home** нawasuhluhk lil bayt bil *arabaya; **do you want to come for a drive?** *a-ıyiz lafa fil *arabaya?; **is it a very long drive?** haya masafa too-weela awee?
driver (of car, bus) sawē'
driver's license rukhsit sawē'a
drive shaft *amood el нaraka
driving licence rukhsit sawē'a
drizzle: it's drizzling bitnadda*
drop: just a drop (of drink) shwıya sooghıyara; **I dropped it** ana wa'*atoo; **drop in some time** eb'a *adee
drought gafaf
drown gheri'; **he's drowning** hoowa beyeghera'
drug (medical) dowa (m); (narcotic) mōkhadaraat
drugstore (for medicines) agzakhēnna; (for general goods) maktabba
drunk (adjective) sakraan
dry (adjective) nashif
dry-clean: can I get these dry-cleaned? muмkin tanadaf dōl *ala e-nashif?

dry-cleaner tandeef *ala e-nashif
duck bata
due: when is the bus due? el ōtōbees gay emta?
dumb (*can't speak*) akhras; (*stupid*) ghebee
dummy (*for baby*) bazaza
dune tal
durex (*tm*) kaboot

during asna'
dust ghoobar
dustbin safeeнet zibella
duty-free (*goods*) bida*a нora
dynamo 'dynamo'
dynasty osra malakaya; **the tenth dynasty** el osra el malakaya el *ashara
dysentery dusuhnteree-a

E

each kul; **each of them** kul waaнid min hum; **one for each of us** waнda lee kul waaнid; **how much are they each?** bikam el waнda?; **each time** kul mara; **we know each other** eнna ne*aruhf ba*d
ear widnuh
earache: I have earache sup*andee waga* fil widnuh
early badree; **early in the morning** e-subн badree; **it's too early** da badree awee; **a day earlier** yum badree; **half an hour earlier** min nus sa*a; **I need an early night** ana lezim anam badree
early riser: I'm an early riser ana dıman uhsнa badree
earring нala'
earth (*soil*) teena
earthenware fokhar
east shar'; **to the east** li shar'
Easter *ıyeed el ayama
easy sehl; **easy with the sugar!** shwıya soogнıara!
eat kal; **I want something to eat** *a-ıyiz нaga akolha; **we've already eaten** eнna kalna
eau-de-Cologne kolonya
eccentric shaaz
edible saleн lil akl
efficient (*hotel, organization*) kofa'
egg bayda

eggplant bitingaana
Egypt masr; **Ancient Egypt** masr el far*onaya
Egyptian (*man, adjective*) masree; (*woman*) masraya
Eire irlanda
either ay; **either ... or ...** ay ... ow ...; **I don't like either of them** ana mabнebbish wala waaнid fee hum
elastic (*noun*) mataat
elastic band astik
Elastoplast (*tm*) shireet laza'
elbow kuwa*
electric bil kaharaba
electric cooker tabaakh kaharabee
electric fire sakhan kaharaba
electrician kaharaba'ee
electricity kaharaba
electric outlet bareeza
elegant sheek
elevator asuhnsayar
else: something else нaga tanee; **somewhere else** нetta tania; **let's go somewhere else** yalla nerooн нetta tania; **what else?** ay tanee?; **nothing else, thanks** bas kedda, shukran
embarrassed maksoof; **he's embarrassed** hoowa maksoof
embarrassing keesoof
embassy safara
emergency tawari'; **this is an emergency** dee нalit tawari'

emery board mabruhd dawafir kartōn

emotional (*person, time*) *atifee

empty faadee

end (*noun*) nehaya; **the end of the film** nehayit el film; **at the end of the road** fil akhr e-taree'; **when does it end?** bit tekhlas emta?

energetic (*person*) nasheet

energy (*of person*) nashaat

engaged (*to be married*) (*woman*) makhtooba; (*man*) khateb; (*toilet, telephone*) masнghool

engagement ring dibla

engine (*car*) mator; (*diesel*) makenna

engineer mohandis

engineering handessa

engine trouble (*car*) *ıyib fil mator

England ingilterra

English ingileezee; **the English** el ingileez; **I'm English** ana ingileezee; (*woman*) ana ingileezaya; **do you speak English?** bititkallim ingileezee?

Englishman ingileezee

Englishwoman ingileezaya

enjoy: I enjoyed it very much *agabnee awee awee; **enjoy yourself!** matta* nafsak!

enjoyable momte*a

enlargement (*of photo*) takbeer

enormous kebeer awee

enough kifaya; **there's not enough** mafeesh kifaya; **it's not big enough** (*too short*) osıyar awee; (*too small*) sooghıyar awee; **it's not enough** mush kifaya; **thank you, that's enough** shukran, da kifaya

entertainment tasslaya

enthusiastic mutaнamis

entrance (*noun*) madkhel

envelope zarf

epileptic musaab bil sara*

equipment mō*ıdet

eraser asteeka

erotic museer

error ghalat

especially khossoosan

espresso coffee ahwa 'espresso'

essential: it is essential that ... da darooree in ...

estate agent simsar

ethnic (*restaurant, clothes*) baladee

Europe orōba

European orōbee

European plan nus ikaama

even: even the English нatta el ingileez; **even if ...** нatta low ...

evening mise'; **good evening** mise' el kheer; **this evening** el layla dee, elleelādee; **in the evening** bil layl

evening meal *asha

evening dress (*for man*) badla smōkin; (*for woman*) foostan sawareh

eventually akheeran

ever: have you ever been to ...? abadan *omruhk roнt li ...?; **if you ever come to Britain** low gayt lingilterra

every kul; **every day** kul yum

everyone kul waaнid

everything kul наga

everywhere kul нetta

exactly! bizobt!

exam imtaнan

example misēl; **for example** masalan

excellent (*food, hotel*) momtaz; **excellent!** momtaz!

except ma*ada; **except Sunday** ma*ada el нad

exception estesna; **as an exception** kuh estesna

excess baggage *afsh zayid

excessive zayid *ala lezoom; **that's a bit excessive** da zeeyada *ala lezoom

exchange (*verb: money*) нowil; **in exchange** badel *an

exchange rate si-a*r e-taнweel; **what's the exchange rate?** bikam si-a*r e-taнweel?

exciting (*day, holiday*) gameel; (*film*) museer

exclusive (*club, hotel*) li tab'a el *allia

excursion reнla ōsıyara; **is there an excursion to ...?** fee reнla lee ...?

excuse me (*to get past*) lowsamaнt; (*to get attention*) min fadlak; (*pardon?*)

ay?; (*annoyed*) lowsamaнt
exhaust (*on car*) e-shakmaan
exhausted (*tired*) mayit min e-ta*b
exhibition ma*ruhd
exist: does it still exist? lessa mowgood?
exit khuroog
expect: I expect so *ala ma-azon; **she's expecting** haya нamil
expensive ghelee
experience tuhgróba; **an absolutely unforgettable experience** tuhgróba matitniseesh
experienced khabeer
expert khabeer
expire: it's expired (*passport etc*) intaha
explain fasuhr; **would you explain that to me?** mumkin tefasuhr da?
explore estakshif; **I just want to go and explore** *a-ıyiz aroон estakshif
export (*verb*) suhduhr
exposure meter mi'yes fatнet el

*adessa
express (*mail*) mista*gil; (*train*) 'express', magaree
extra: can we have an extra chair? mumkin korsee tanee?; **is that extra?** (*in cost*) da zeeyada?
extraordinarily: extraordinarily beautiful gameel awee awee awee
extraordinary (*very strange*) ghereeb giddan
extremely awee awee; **that's extremely expensive** da ghelee awee awee
extrovert monbuhsit
eye *ın (*f*); **will you keep an eye on my bags for me?** mumkin tekhellee baalak min e-shónuht?
eyebrow нawagib (*f*)
eyebrow pencil alam нawagib
eye drops atra lil *ın
eyeliner koнl
eye shadow zil lil *ıyoon
eye witness shehid

F

fabulous khoorafee
face wish
face mask (*for driving*) nuhdaarit ghóts
face pack (*cosmetic*) 'mask'
facing: facing the sea ódam el baнr
fact нa'ee'a
factory masna*
Fahrenheit 'fahrenheit'; *see page 119*
faint: she's fainted óghma *alayha; **I'm going to faint** нıyughma *alaya
fair (*fun-fair*) moolid; (*commercial*) ma*rad; **it's not fair** da mush *adl; **OK, fair enough** mashee khalas
fake ta'leed
fall wi'ya*; **he's had a fall** hoowa wi'ya*; **he fell off his bike** wi'ya* min *ala el *agala; **in the fall**

(*autumn*) fil khareef
false muzayif
false teeth ta'm asnan
family *ıayla
family name ism el ıayla
famished: I'm famished ana mayit min e-gooa*
famous mashhoor
fan (*mechanical, hand-held*) marawaнa; (*football etc*) mushaga*a
fan belt sayuhr el marawaнa
fancy mo*gabee; **he fancies you** hoowa mo*gab beekee
fantastic modhish
far ba*yeed; **is it far?** da ba*yeed?; **how far is it to ...?** el masefa dee ay lee ...?; **as far as I'm concerned** binesbaalee

fare ōgra; **what's the fare to ...?** el ōgra kam lee ...?

farm *azba

farther ab*ad; **farther than ...** ab*ad min ...

fashion (*in clothes etc*) mōda

fashionable akher mōda

fast saree-a*; **not so fast** mush bisora*a

fast (*noun*) seeyaam; **are you fasting?** inta sıyim?

fastener (*zip*) sosta

faster/fastest asra*

fat (*person*) tekheen; (*on meat*) simeen

father ab; **my father** abooya

father-in-law (*father of wife*) aboo el madam; (*fatheer of husband*) aboo gooz

fathom arar

fattening disim

faucet Hanafaya

fault zamb; **it was my fault** da zambee ana; **it's not my fault** mush zambee ana

faulty (*equipment*) fee *ıyib

favo(u)rite mazeg; **that's my favo(u)rite** da mazēgee

fawn (*colour*) bonee asfar fete*H

February fibrıuhr

fed up: I'm fed up ana zah'en; **I'm fed up with ...** ana zah'en min ...

feeding bottle ezazzit reeda*a

feel: I feel hot ana Haraan; **I feel cold** ana sa'*an; **I feel like a drink** *a-ıyiz ashrab Haga; **I don't feel like it** (*doing something*) maleesh mazeg; (*food, drink*) maleesh nifs; **how are you feeling today?** izzay saHetuhk e-naharda?; **I'm feeling a lot better** ana Hassis bitaHassun

fence soor

fender (*of car*) ekseedaam

ferry ma*daya; **what time's the last ferry?** emta akher ma*daya?

festival mahragaan

fetch gēb; **I'll go and fetch it** ana HarooH ageeboo; **will you come and fetch me?** mumkin teegee tekhudnee?

fever Humaa

feverish: I'm feeling feverish ana Hassis bee sukhunaya

few shwıya; **only a few** shwıya bas; **a few minutes** da'ay'; **he's had a good few** (*to drink*) shirib keteer

fiancé: my fiancé khateebee

fiancée: my fiancée khatibtee

fiasco: what a fiasco! karsa!

field ghayt

fifty-fifty nus-nus

fight (*noun*) khina'a

figs teen

figure (*of person*) kasm; (*number*) *adad; **I have to watch my figure** ana lezim aHafiz *ala kasmee

fill mala; **fill her up please** imlaha lowsamaHt; **will you help me fill out this form?** mumkin tesa*adnee amla e-namoozag da?

fillet shareeHa

filling (*in tooth*) Hashw; **it's very filling** (*food*) da yishaba* awee

filling station maHattit benzeen

film (*in cinema, for camera*) film; **do you have this type of film?** *andak nooa* el film da?; **16mm film** film sittaashar millee; **35mm film** film khamsa wi talaateen millee

filter (*for camera, coffee*) filtuhr

filter-tipped bi filtuhr

filthy (*room etc*) wisikh

find le'eh; **I can't find it** mush le'eeh; **if you find it** low le'it-hoo; **I've found a ...** ana le'eet ...

fine kwıyis; **that's fine** da kwıyis; **I'm fine** ana kwıyis; **it's fine weather** gow gameel; **how are you? — fine thanks** izzayak? — kwıyis; **a 30 pound fine** talaateen ginay ghuhrama

finger sooba*

fingernail dofr e-sooba*

finish khalas; **I haven't finished** lessa makhalastish; **when I've finished** lama khalas; **when does it finish?** bitakhlas emta?; **finish off your drink** khalas mashroobuhk

fire narr (*f*); **fire!** (*i.e. something's on*

fire) Haree'a!; **may we light a fire here?** mumkin noowala* narr hena?; **it's on fire** moowala*a; **it's not firing properly** (*car*) el mator bee'uhta*

fire alarm garuhs inzar

fire brigade, fire department el mataafee

fire escape makhruhg

fire extinguisher tafiet Haree'a

firm (*company*) shirka; **my firm** shirkitee

first owel; **I was first** ana kunt el owel; **at first** awalan; **this is the first time** dee owel mara

first aid issa*af awalee

first aid kit shantit iss*af awalee

first class (*travel etc*) darga oola

first name ism

fish (*noun*) samak

fisherman sayad samak

fishing sayid e-samak

fishing boat markib sayid

fishing net shabakit sayid samak

fishing rod sinara

fishing tackle *Idit sayid samak

fishing village kareeyit sayid samak

fit (*healthy*) layi'; **I'm not very fit** ma*ndeesh lee ye'a; **he's a keep fit fanatic** hoowa mazegoo el leeye'a; **it doesn't fit** mush monasib

fix: can you fix it? mumkin tessalHoo?; **let's fix a time** yalla niHadid ma*ad; **it's all fixed up** kuloo tamem; **I'm in a bit of a fix** ana fee mowkif moHrig

fizzy fowarr

fizzy drink mashroob fowarr

flab (*on body*) simeen

flag *alam

flannel (*face*) foota; (*fabric*) fanilla

flash (*for camera*) 'flash'

flashlight battaraya

flashy (*clothes etc*) Iyim

flat (*adjective*) moosataH; **this beer is flat** el beera dee mush kwIyissa; **I've got a flat tyre/tire** el kawetsh nayim; (*apartment*) sha'a

flatterer monafi'

flatware (*cutlery*) fuhdeeyaat; (*crockery*) fokhar

flavo(u)r ta*am

flea barghoot

flea bite arsit barghoot

flea powder budrit barragheet

flexible (*material, arrangements*) marin

flies (*on trousers*) fatHet el bantalon

flight tIyara

flippers za*anif

flirt dalel

float *awema

flood fIadaan

floor (*of room*) ard (*f*); **on the floor** *alel ard; **on the second floor** (*UK*) fidor e-taalit; (*US*) fidor e-tanee

floorshow *ard

flop (*failure*) fashal

florist maHal zuhor

flour di'ee'

flower zahra

flu infilwenza

fluent tuhlee'; **he speaks fluent Arabic** hoowa bikellim *arabee beetuhla'a

fly (*verb*) tarr; **can we fly there?** mumkin nerooH bi tIyara?

fly (*insect*) dibana

fly spray bakhakhit diban

fog shabora; **it's foggy** e-gow shabora

fog lights noor li shabora

folk dancing ra's folkloree

folk music mooseeka sha*baya; (*in Upper Egypt*) mooseeka suhI-eedee

follow tebe*a; **follow me** tabe*anee

fond: I'm quite fond of ... ana moghruhm bee ...

food akl; **the food's excellent** el akl momtaz

food poisoning tassamum

food store maHal bee'ala

fool ghebee

foolish ghebee

foot rigl; **on foot** *ala e-riglayn; *see page 117*

football (*game, ball*) kora kuhduhm

for *alashen; **is that for me?** da *alashenee?; **what's this for?** da *alashen ay?; **for two days** limodit yoomayn; **I've been here for a week**

ana ba'alee hena isboo*a; **a bus for ... ō**tōbees lee ...

forbidden mamnoo-a* *(strictly and religiously)* Haraam; **is it forbidden?** da Haraam?

forehead oora

foreign agnabee

foreigner *(man)* agnabee; *(woman)* agnabaya

foreign exchange *(money)* taHweel *omla

forget nessee; **I forget, I've forgotten** niseet; **don't forget** matinsash

fork *(for eating)* shoka; *(in road)* tafare*a

form *(in hotel, to fill out)* namoozag

formal *(dress)* Heshma; *(person)* dōghree; *(language)* rasmaya

fortnight isboo*ayn

fortress al*a

fortunately lay Hosn el Haz

fortune-teller *araf

forward: could you forward my mail? mumkin teba*t gowabatee *ala el *Inwān e-gedeed?

forwarding address el *Inwān e-gedeed

foundation cream 'cream' Himaya

fountain *(ornamental)* nafora; *(for drinking)* Hanafaya

foyer *(of hotel, theatre)* saala

fracture *(noun)* sha'

fractured skull gomgomma mash'oo'a

fragile sahl el kasr

frame *(for picture)* biroo-ez

France faransa

fraud nasb

free *(at liberty)* HoHr; *(costing nothing)* bi balash; **admission free** e-dikhool bi balash

freezer frayzuhr

freezing cold bard awee awee

French *(adjective, language)* fransaawee

French fries batates maHamara

frequent *alatool

fresh *(weather, breeze)* mon*esh; *(fruit*

etc) taaza; *(cheeky)* sehee; **don't get fresh with me** mat-Howelsh ma*aya

fresh orange juice *aseer bortooa'n taaza

friction tape shireet *Izil

Friday el gom*a

fridge talaga

fried egg bayda ma'laya

friend saHib

friendly Hebbee

frog dovd*a

from min; **I'm from London** ana min 'london'; **from here to the sea** min hena lil baHr; **the next boat from ...** el markib e-gay min ...; **as from Tuesday** min yum e-talaat

front wag-ha; **in front** ōdam; **in front of us** ōdamna; **at the front** fil mō'dimma

frozen migammid; **frozen food** akl migammid

fruit fawaki

fruit juice *aseer fawaki

fruit salad salatit fawaki

frustrating moHIyar; **it's very frustrating** moHIyar awee

fry *(vegetables)* Hamar; *(fish)* ala; **nothing fried** wala Haga ma'laya

frying pan taasa

full malyan; **it's full of ...** malyan bee ...; **I'm full** *(eating)* ana shaba*an

full-board ikaama kamla

fun mōt*a; **it's fun** da mōt*a; **it was great fun** kan momte*a; **just for fun** li taslaya; **have fun** mata* nafsak

funeral ganaza

funny *(strange)* ghereeb; *(amusing)* fookehee

furniture asses

further aba*d; **2 kilometres further** ba*d itneen kiloomitr; **further down the road** ōdam shwIya

fuse: the lights have fused e-noor darab

fuse wire silk musahir

future moost'abil; **in future** fil moost'abil

G

gale *asifa
gallon *see page 119*
gallstones el Haswa e-suhfra
gamble aamir; I don't gamble ana
maleesh fil ōmar
game le*aba
games room saalit el le*ab
garage (*petrol*) maHattit benzeen; (*repair*) warshit *arabeeyaat; (*for parking*) mow'af *arabeeyaat
garbage zibella
garden goonayna
garlic tōm
gas ghez; (*gasoline*) benzeen
gas cylinder (*for Calor gas*) anboobit bootagaz
gasket takhsheena
gas pedal dawāset el benzeen
gas station maHattit benzeen
gas tank khazan benzeen
gastroenteritis eltihab fil masareen
gate (*also at airport*) bewābba
gauge mi'yes
gay (*homosexual*) khawal
gear tirs; the gears keep sticking e-tuhroos bititzini' ma*a ba*daha
gearbox sandoo' e-tuhroos; I have gearbox trouble fee *Iyib fee sandoo' e-tuhroos
gear lever, gear shift *asIyit el fitis
gekko seHlaya
general delivery *you have a post box number:* sandoo' bareed rakuhm
generous kareem; that's very generous of you da karuhm kebeer minak
gentleman (*man*) moHtaram; that gentleman over there el akh el moHtaram ellee hinak; he's such a gentleman hoowa moHtaram giddan
gents (*toilet*) tawalet rigālee

genuine Ha'ee'ee
German measles el Hazba el almanaya
Germany almanya
get: have you got ...? (*in a shop*) *andak ...?, fee ...?; (*said to a woman*) *andik ...?; have you got my address? ma*ak *Inwānee?; how do I get to ...? izzay arooH lil ...?; where do I get it from? *ageeboo minayn?; can I get you a drink? teshrab ay?; will you get it for me? mumkin tigibhoolee?; when do we get there? Hanoosal emta?; I've got to ... ana lezim ...; I've got to go ana lezim amshee; where do I get off? anzil fayn?; it's difficult to get to sa*ab el wisool lee; when I get up (*in morning*) lama asHa
ghastly fazee-a*
ghost shabaH
giddy dayekh; it makes me giddy bekhaleenee adōkh
gift hidaya
gigantic dakhm
gin sHin; a gin and tonic sHin wee tonik
girl bint
girlfriend saHibitee
give edda; will you give me ...? mumkin teddeenee ...?; I'll give you one pound Hadeeluk ginay; I gave it to him ana eddit-hooloo; will you give it back? mumkin terega*oo?; would you give this to ...? mumkin teddee da lee ...?
glad mabsoot
glamorous (*woman*) fatenna
gland ghoda
glandular fever Homa fil ghodad
glass (*material*) eezez; (*for drinking*)

koobaya; **a glass of water** koobayit mıya
glasses (*spectacles*) nuhdara
gloves gawantee
glue (*noun*) samgh
gnat namoosa
go raн; **we want to go to ...** *ızeen nerooн lee ...; **I'm going there tomorrow** ana rıaн hinak bukra; **when does it go?** (*bus etc*) beeyetla* emta?; **where are you going?** inta rıaн fayn?; **let's go** yalla nimshee; **he's gone** hoowa mishee; **it's all gone** khalaas; **I went there yesterday** ana roнt hinak imbarraн; **go away!** imshee!; **it's gone off** (*milk etc*) fēhsid; **we're going out tonight** eнna khargeen e-layla dee; **do you want to go out tonight?** *a-ıyiz tukhrug e-layla dee?; **has the price gone up?** e-tamen zād?
goal (*sport*) gōn
goat me*aza
goat's cheese gibnit m*ı-eez
God allah; **God willing** inshah' allah
god illah
goddess illaha
gold dahab
golf 'golf'
golf clubs *asıyit el golf
golf course malab el golf
good kwıyis; **good!** kwıyis!; **that's no good** da mush kwıyis; **good heavens!** allahoo akbar!
goodbye ma*asalemma
good-looking (*man*) damoo khafeef; (*woman*) damaha khafeef
gooey (*food etc*) milaza' wimsuhkar
goose wizza
gorgeous gameel
government нōkooma
gradually shwıya shwıya
grammar *alm e-naнw
gram(me) giraam; *see page 117*
granddaughter нafeeda
grandfather gid
grandmother gidda
grandson нafeed
granny nayna

grapefruit graybfroot
grapefruit juice *aseer graybfroot
grapes *ınab; (*small, seedless*) *ınab banātee; (*large, sweet, brown*) *ınab fayoomee
grass (*on lawn, drug*) нasheesh
grateful mootshēkir; **I'm very grateful to you** ana mootshēkir giddan
gravy dima*a
gray roomaadee
grease (*for car*) shaнm; (*on food*) dehn
greasy (*food*) dehnee
great *azeem; **that's great!** da *azeem!
Great Britain ingilterra
Greece el yoonan
greedy tama*
green akhdar
greengrocer khōdaree
grey roomaadee
grilled mashwee
gristle (*on meat*) ar'oosha
grocer ba'ēl
ground ard (*f*); **on the ground** *alel ard; **on the ground floor** fil dōhr el ardee
ground beef laнma mafrooma
group magmoo*a
group insurance ta'meen
group leader rıyis
guarantee (*noun*) damaan; **is it guaranteed?** da *alay damaan?
guardian (*of child*) walay el umr
guest dayif
guesthouse benseeyōn
guest room ōdit e-zoo-war
guide (*noun*) morshid
guidebook daleel siyāнee
guilty mōgrim
guitar 'guitar'
Gulf States el khaleeg el *arabee
gum lessa; (*chewing gum*) liban
gun bundoo'aya
gymnasium saalit e-reeyada el badanaya
gyn(a)ecologist akhissaa'ee uhmraad nissa
gypsum gibs

H

hair sha*r
hairbrush forshit sha*r
haircut uhs e-sha*r; **just an ordinary haircut please** uhs baseet lowsamaнt
hairdresser kowafayar
hairdryer eksishwar
hair gel 'gel' li sha*r
hair grip bensit sha*r; (*with fancy decoration*) tooka
hair lacquer lakay lil sha*r
hair style: have you got a catalogue of hairstyles? *andik 'catalogue'?
half nus; **half an hour** nus sa*a; **half a litre/liter** nus litr; **half as much** nusi da; **half as much again** nusi da kamem
halfway: halfway to Cairo fee nus e-sikka lil kaheera
hamburger 'hamburger'
hammer (*noun*) shakoosh
hand eed; **hands** eedayn; **will you give me a hand?** mumkin tesa*adnee?
handbag shantit eed
hand baggage shanta
handbrake faraamil eed
handkerchief mandeel
handle (*noun*) okra; **will you handle it?** mumkin te*amiloo?
hand luggage shanta
handmade sōna* yadawee
handsome damoo khafeef
hanger (*for clothes*) shama*a
hangover suda*; **I've got a terrible hangover** *andee suda* shedeed
happen hassal; **how did it happen?** Hassal izzay?; **what's happening?** ay ellee beyaнsal?; **it won't happen again** mush Hate-aнsal tanee
happy mabsoot; **we're not happy with the room** eнna mush

mo*agabeen bil ōda
harbo(u)r meena
hard gamid; (*difficult*) sa*b
hard-boiled egg bayda masloo-a awee
hardly (*with difficulty*) biso*ooba; **hardly ever** nadir; **there's hardly any left** mafeesh keteer
hardware store maнal adawet manzilaya
harem Hareem
harm (*noun*) azaya
hassle: it's too much hassle kuloo mata*ıb; **a hassle-free trip** reнla bidoon mata*ıb
hat ta'aya
hate: I hate ... ana bakra ...
have: do you have ...? (*in a shop etc*) *andak ...?, fee ...?; (*said to a woman*) *andik ...?; **do you have any money?** ma*ak feloos?; **can I have ...?** mumkin ...?; **can I have some water?** mumkin shwıyit mıya?; **I have ...** *andee ...; **I don't have ...** ma*andeesh ...; **can we have breakfast in our room?** mumkin neftar fee ōditna?; **have another** medeeduhk; **I have to leave early** ana lezim amshee badree; **do I have to ...?** ana lezim ...?; **do we have to ...?** eнna lezim ...?; *see page 114*
hay fever zookam rabee*ı
he hoowa; **is he here?** hoowa hena?; **where does he live?** hoowa sekin fayn?; *see page 106*
head ras (*f*); **we're heading for Aswan** eнna rıнeen aswaan
headache suda*
headgear kiswuh li ras
headlights e-noor el amāmee
headphones sama*at
headscarf asharb

headsquare (*large traditional*) talfeeнa
head waiter ra'ees el garsonat
head wind ree-aн *aksaya
health seнa; **your health!**
fiseнuhtuhk!
healthy (*person, food, climate*) seнee
hear simea*; **can you hear me?** te'dar
tisma*nee?; **I can't hear you** ana
mush sam*ak; **I've heard about it**
seema*t *anha
hearing aid sama*it widn
heart alb
heart attack zabнa sadraya
hearts (*cards*) kōba
heat нarara; **not in this heat!** mush
fil нarr da!
heater (*in car*) sakhen
heating tadfi'a
heat rash нamoneel
heat stroke darbit shams
heatwave mogit нarr
heavy ti'eel
hectic lakhbuhtta
heel (*of foot, of shoe*) ka*b; **could you
put new heels on these?** mumkin
terakibluhum ka*b gedeed?
heelbar tuhsleeyeн gizzam
height *ıloo
helicopter 'helicopter'
hell: oh hell! e-la*na!; **go to hell!**
rooн fi daheeya!
hello ahlan; (*in surprise*) mish
ma*ool!; (*on phone*) allō
helmet (*for motorcycle*) khooza
help (*verb*) seh*ıd; **can you help me?**
mumkin tesa*ıdnee?; **thanks for
your help** shukran; **help!** нa'oonee!
helpful: he was very helpful hoowa
kan mufeed awee; **that's helpful** da
mufeed awee
helping: can I have another helping?
mumkin tanee?
henna нenna
hepatitis eltihab fil kibd
her: I don't know her ana
ma*rafhaash; **will you send it to
her?** mumkin teb*at-helha?; **it's her**
dee haya; **with her** ma*aha; **for her**
*alashēnha: **her house** bayt-ha; **her**

husband goozha; **that's her suitcase**
dee shantit-ha; *see pages 105, 106*
herbs a*asheb
here hena; **here you are** (*giving something*) itfuhduhl; **here he comes**
hoowa gay
hers bita*ha; **that's hers** da bita*ha;
see page 108
hey! (*to a man*) inta!; (*to a woman*)
intee!
hi! 'hi!'
hibiscus karkaday
hiccups zooghotta
hide istakhaba
hideous fazee-a*
hieroglyphics hıroghleefaya
high *alee
highbeam e-noor el *alee
highchair korsee *alee
highway taree' sareeya*
hill matla*; **it's further up the hill**
shwıya fo' el matla*
hillside gamb el matla*
hilly kuloo matale-a*
him: I don't know him ana
ma*rafhoosh; **will you send it to
him?** mumkin teb*at-hooloo; **it's
him** da hoowa; **with him** ma*ah; **for
him** *alashēnoo; *see page 106*
hip hunsh
hire uhguhr; **can I hire a car?**
mumkin a-uhguhr *arabaya?; **do
you hire them out?** inta
bituhguhrhum?
his: his house baytoo; **his wife**
miraatoo; **it's his drink** da
mashrooboo; **it's his** da bita*oo; *see
pages 105, 108*
history tareekh; **the history of the
Pharaohs** tareekh el fara*ana
hit darab; **he hit me** hoowa darabnee;
I hit my head ana khabat rasee
hitch: is there a hitch? fee нaga?
hit record oghnaya mush-hora
hole khorum
holiday agēzza; **I'm on holiday** ana fi
agēzza
Holland hollanda
home bayt; **at home** (*in my house etc*)

fil bayt; (*in my country*) fi baladee; **I
go home tomorrow** ana marowaн
bukra
home address *ınwān el bayt
homemade baytee; (*made in the shop
etc*) maнallee
homesick: I'm homesick ana mushte'
arga* lee baladee
honest ameen
honestly? Ha'ee?
honey *asal naнl
honeymoon shahr el *asal; **we are on
our honeymoon** eнna fi shahr el
*asal
hood (*of car*) kaboot
hoover (*tm*) maknassa bil kaharaba
hope amal; **I hope so** atmana haza; **I
hope not** matmanash
horn (*of car*) kalaks; (*of animal*) arn
horrible mor*ıb
hors d'oeuvre mazzah
horse hossaan
horse riding rikoob el kheel
hose (*for car radiator*) кhartum mıya
hospital mustashfa
hospitality karam; **thank you for
your hospitality** shukran *ala
karamak
hostel mo*askuhr shebab
hot sukhn; (*curry etc*) Hamee; **I'm
hot** ana Haraan; **something hot
to eat** Haga sukhna akulha; **it's
so hot today** e-gow Harr awee

e-naharda
hotel fondō'; **at my hotel** fil fondō'
hotel clerk (*receptionist*) moo-wazuhf
isti'bel
hotplate (*on cooker*) 'hotplate'
hour sa*a; **on the hour** kul sa*a
house bayt
housewife rabit bayt
house wine nebeez maнallee
how izzay; **how many?** ad'ay?; **how
much?** bikam?; **how often?** kul
ad'ay?; **how are you?** (*to a man*)
izzayak?; (*to a woman*) izzayik?; **how
do you do?** (*to a man*) izzayak?; (*to a
woman*) izzayik?; **how about a beer?**
teshrab beera?; **how nice!** fekra
momtaza!; **would you show me how
to?** mumkin tewarreenee?
humid moratuhb
humidity rotooba
**humo(u)r: where's your sense of
humo(u)r?** fayn soobak el fookehee?
hundredweight *see page 118*
hungry: I'm hungry ana ga*an; **I'm
not hungry** ana mush ga*an
hurry: I'm in a hurry ana mista*gil;
hurry up! yalla bisora*a!; **there's no
hurry** *ala mahlak
hurt: it hurts bitooga*; **my back
hurts** dahree beeyooga*nee
husband zog; **my husband** goozee
hydro-electric кahroomē'ee
hydrofoil luhnsh muhtaat, 'hydrofoil'

I

I ana; **I am English** (*man*) ana
ingileezee; (*woman*) ana ingileezaya;
I live in Manchester ana *ı-ish
fee 'manchester'; *see page 106*
ice talg; **with ice** bi talg; **with ice and
lemon** bi talg wi lamoon
ice cream 'ice cream', sнelatee
ice-cream cone 'ice cream' fee

baskoot
ice lolly lollee-uhb
idea fikra; **good idea!** fikra kwıyissa!
ideal (*solution, time*) missēlee
identity papers owra'a shakhsaya
idiot ghebee
idyllic gazāb
if low; **if you could** low te'dar; **if not**

low la'a
ignition marsh
ill *ıyēn; **I feel ill** ana *ıyēn
illegal gheer shar*ı
illegible mush waadeн
illness marad
imitation (*leather etc*) te'leed
immediately нālan
immigration hegra
import (*verb*) estowrid
important mōhim; **it's very
important** da mōhim awee; **it's not
important** da mush mōhim
impossible mustaнeel
impressive mo'assir
improve: it's improving bitit-нassin;
I want to improve my Arabic ana
*a-ıyiz aнassin el *arabee bita*ee
improvement taнseen
in fee; **in my room** fee ōtee; **in the
town centre** fee west el balad; **in
Cairo** fil kaheera; **in London** fee
'london'; **in one hour's time** fee
mōdit sa*a; **in August** fee aghostos;
in English bil ingileezee; **in Arabic**
bil *arabee; **is he in?** hoowa
mowgood?
inch boosa; *see page 117*
**include: is that included in the
price?** da maнsoob fi se*ar?
incompetent khayb
inconvenient mush moola'im
increase (*noun*) zeeyāda
incredible (*very good, amazing*)
mōdhish
indecent aleel el adab
independent нorr
India el hind
Indian (*man, adjective*) hindee;
(*woman*) hindaya
Indian Ocean el mōнeet el hindee
indicator (*on car*) noor eeshaara
indigestion soo' hadam
indoor pool нammem sibaнa shitwee
indoors gowa
industry sina*a
inefficient mush kwıyis
infection *adwa
infectious mo*adee

inflammation eltihab
inflation tadakhum
informal (*clothes, occasion, meeting*)
mush rasmee
information ma*lōmat
information desk esta*lamat
information office maktab el
esta*lamat
injection но'na
injured insaab; **she's been injured**
haya insaabit
injury eesaaba
innocent baree'a
inquisitive fidoolee
insect нashara
insect bite arsit нashara
insecticide moobeed lil нasharaat
insect repellent taarid lil нasharaat
inside: inside the tent fil
khayma; **let's sit inside** yalla no'a*d
gowa
insincere mush ameen
insist: I insist ana muser
insomnia aruhk
instant coffee 'nescafe'
instead badal; **I'll have that one instead** ana нekhud da aнsen; **instead
of ...** badal min ...; **can we go to
Luxor instead of Aswan?** mumkin
nerooн lu'sor badal min aswaan?
insulating tape shireet *ızil
insulin 'insulin'
insult (*noun*) eehāna
insurance ta'meen; **write your insurance company here** ekitb ism shirkit
ta'meenak hena
insurance policy boleesit ta'meen
intellectual (*noun*) musakuhf
intelligent zakee
intentional: it wasn't intentional
makensh ma'sood
interest: places of interest amakin lil
mota*a
interested: I'm very interested in ...
ana mohtam awee bee ...
interesting mumtea*; **that's very
interesting** da mumtea* awee
international *alemmee
international driving licence rokhsit

sawē'a dowlaya
interpret targim; **would you interpret?** mumkin tetergim?
interpreter motergim
intersection (*crossroads*) ta'aata* turo'
interval (*during play etc*) estiraнa
into lil; **I'm not into that** (*don't like*)
ana mabaнebboosh
introduce: may I introduce ...?
mumkin a*rafuhk ...?
introvert montaawee
invalid (*not legal*) baatil; (*noun: person*)
*ıyēn
invalid chair korsee lil *agazuh
invitation (*general*) da*wa; (*for meal*)
*ızooma; **thank you for the invitation** shukran *ala e-da*wa; **thank
you for the dinner invitation**
shukran *ala el *ızooma
invite da*a; **can I invite you out?**
mumkin a*zimak bara?
**involved: I don't want to get in-
volved in it** ana mush *a-ıyiz
adakhil
iodine sabghityood
Iran iraan
Iranian (*man,* *adjective*) iraanee;
(*woman*) iraanaya

Iraq el *ıra'
Iraqi *ıra'ee
Ireland irlanda
Irish irlandee
Irishman irlandee
Irishwoman irlandaya
iron (*material*) нadeed; (*for clothes*)
makwa; **can you iron these for me?**
mumkin tekwee dōl *alashēnee?
ironmonger maнal adawet manzillaya
irrigation e-rı
is *see page 113*
Islam el islam
island gezeera
isolated ma*zool
Israel isra-eel
Israeli isra-eelee
it (*for masculine nouns*) da; (*for feminine
nouns*) dee; **is it ...?** da/dee?; **where
is it?** fayn da/dee?; **it's her** dee
haya; **it was ...** kan ...; **that's just it**
(*just the problem*) dee el mushkilla;
that's it (*that's right*) saн!; *see page
106*
Italy ituhlya
itch: it itches bitakulnee
itinerary khat e-reнla

J

jack (*for car*) sнak; (*cards*) walad
jacket sнakit
jam (*preserve*) mirabuh; **apricot jam**
mirabit mishmish; **a traffic jam**
zaнmit maroor; **I jammed on the
brakes** dosta *ala el faraamil
January yanaayuhr
jaundice marad e-suhfruh
jasmine yasmeen
jaw fak
jazz mooseeka el sнaz
jealous ghıyoor; **he's jealous** hoowa
ghıyoor

jeans sнeenz
jellyfish samak hoolāmee
jerboa far el ghayit
Jerusalem el ods
jetty raseef
Jew (*man,* *adjective*) yahoodee; (*woman*)
yahoodaya
jewel(le)ry moogowharaat
Jewish yahoodee
jiffy: just a jiffy estanna shwiya
job shoghl; **just the job!** (*just right*) da
tamam; **it's a good job you told me!**
kwıyis ellee inta oltillee

jog: I'm going for a jog ana гıaн
agree
jogging garee-y
join: I'd like to join ana *a-ıyiz
eltaнuh'; can I join you? (go with)
mumkin aroон ma*ak; (sit with)
mumkin a*od ma*ak?; do you want
to join us? (go with) *a-ıyiz teegee
ma*ana?; (sit with) *a-ıyiz to'a*od
ma*ana?
joint (in body) mufasalla; (to smoke)
нasheesh
joke nokta; you've got to be joking!
inta lezim bitnakit!; it's no joke dee
mush nokta
joker 'joker'
jolly: it was jolly good kan нelw
awee; jolly good! нelw awee!
Jordan el ordun
Jordanian (man, adjective) ordōnee;
(woman) ordōnaya
journey reнla; have a good journey!
reнla sa*ıeeda!; safe journey!
tewoosal bi salemma!
jug abree'; a jug of water shafsha'
mıya
July yulya
jump nuht; you made me jump
inta khadetnee; jump in! (to car)
erkab!
jumper bullōvuhr
jump leads, jumper cables kablēt
junction takaata*
June yoonya
junior: Mr Ahmed junior el ōstez
ahmed el sooghıyar
junk (rubbish) zibella
just: just one waaнid bas; just me
ana bas; just for me laya ana bas;
just a little shwıya sooghıyara; just
here bas hena; not just now mush
delwa'tee; that's just right da taman;
it's just as good da yenfa*; he was
here just now hoowa kan hena
delwa'tee; I've only just arrived ana
lessa waasil delwa'tee

K

kebab kebab
keen: I'm not keen maleesh mazeg
keep: can I keep it? mumkin
akhaleeh?; please keep it khalee
ma*ak; keep the change khalee el
be'ee; will it keep? (food) нat*ı-
eesh?; it's keeping me awake
mikhaleenee saaнee; it keeps on
breaking dıman tetkessir; I can't
keep anything down (food) ana
batrush aya нaga
kerb raseef
kerosene gas
ketchup 'ketchup'
kettle baraad
key muftaн
kid: the kids el *ıyēl; I'm not
kidding ana mush banakit
kidneys (body) killa; (food) kallawee
kill atal
kilo keeloo; see page 118
kilometre, kilometer keeloomitr; see
page 117
kind: that's very kind da zo' minak;
this kind of ... nōa* el ...; I don't
like this kind of food ana
mabaнebbish nōa* el akl da
king malik; (cards) shayib
kiosk koshk
kiss (noun) boosa; (verb) bes
kitchen mutbukh
kitchenette mutbukh sooghıyar
Kleenex (tm) kliniks
knee rukba
kneecap saboonit e-rukba
knickers kulotēt нareemee

knife sikeena
knitting (*act, material*) tereekō
knitting needles ebar tereekō
knock: there's a knocking noise from the engine fee khabuht fil mator; **he's had a knock on the head** hoowa etkhabuht *ala deemeghoo; **he's been knocked over** hoowa we'a*
knot (*in rope*) *a'oda
know (*somebody, something*) *arif; **I**

don't know ma*arafsh; **do you know a good restaurant?** te*araf mat*am kwɪyiz?; **who knows?** ma*arafsh; **I didn't know that** ana ma*areftish da; **I don't know him** ana ma*arafoosh
Koran kur'aan
Kuwait koowayt
Kuwaiti (*man, adjective*) koowaytee; (*woman*) koowaytaya

L

label tikit
laces (*for shoes*) roobaat gazma
lacquer (*for hair*) lakay
ladies (room) tawalet
lady madam; **ladies and gentlemen!** sayidatee saadatee!
lager stella (*tm*)
lake birka
lamb (*meat*) daanee; (*animal*) oozee
lamp lamba
lamppost *amood e-noor
lampshade abasHora
land (*not sea*) ard (*f*); **when does the plane land?** e-tɪyara Hatewoosal emta?
lane (*small street*) Haara; (*a country lane*) zira*ee
language logha
language course kors logha
large kebeer
laryngitis eltihab fil Huhngara
last akheer; **last year** e-sana ellee fatit; **last Wednesday** el arba* ellee fat; **last week** el isboo-a* ellee fat; **last night** lilt-imbarraH; **when's the last bus?** akheer ōtōbees emta?; **one last drink** akheer waaHid; **when were you last in London?** emta kunt akheer mara fi 'london'?; **at last!** akheeran!; **how long does it last?**

bitakhud ad ay?
last name ism el *ɪla
late mitaakhuhr; **sorry I'm late** asif *ala takheer; **don't be late** matitakharsh; **the bus was late** el ōtōbees kan mitaakhuhr; **we'll be back late** Hanerga* mitaakhuhr; **it's getting late** el wa't etakhuhr; **is it that late!** dee saHeeH wakhree?; **it's too late now** el wa't mitaakhuhr delwa'tee; **I'm a late riser** ana dɪman uhsHa mitakhur
lately min moda; **I haven't seen him lately** ana mashuftoosh min moda
later ba*dayn; **later on** ba*dayn; **I'll come back later** ana Harga* tanee; **see you later** ashoofak; **no later than Tuesday** lezim abl yum e-talaat
latest: the latest news akher akhbar; **at the latest** mush ba*d
laugh daHek; **don't laugh** matetHaksh; **it's no laughing matter** dee Haga madaHaksh
launderette, laundromat maghsalla afrangee
laundry (*clothes*) gheseel; (*place*) maghsalla; **could you get the laundry done?** mumkin teghsil el hidoom?
lavatory tawalet

law kaanoon; **against the law** duhd el kaanoon

lawn ard Hasheesh (f)

lawyer moHāmee

laxative mullayin

laze around: I just want to laze around mush *a-ɪyiz a*mil Haga

lazy kaslān; **don't be lazy** mateba'sh kaslān; **a nice lazy holiday** agezza hadee-a

lead (electrical) silk kaharaba; **where does this road lead?** e-taree' da yoo-wedee fayn?

leaf wara'

leaflet matboo-a*; **do you have any leaflets on ...?** fee matboo*aat *ala ...?

leak rashaH; **the roof leaks** esa'af beeyershaH

learn daras; **I want to learn ...** ana *a-ɪyiz adris ...

learner: I'm just a learner ana lessa mobtadi'

lease (verb) uhguhr

least: not in the least etlaakuhn; **at least 50** khamseen *alel a'al

leather gild

leave: when does the bus leave? el ōtōbees beeyetla* emta?; **I leave tomorrow** ana mashee bukra; **he left this morning** hoowa mishee e-subH; **may I leave this here?** mumkin esseeb da hena?; **I left my bag in the bar** ana sebt shantitee fil bar; **she left her bag here** haya sebit shantit-ha hena; **leave the window open please** seeb e-shebek maftooH lowsamaHt; **there's not much left** mafeesh keteer; **I've hardly any money left** ma*yeesh feloos keteer; **I'll leave it up to you** inta tekarar

Lebanese (man, adjective) libnānee; (woman) libnanaya

Lebanon libnan

lecherous shahwēnee

left shimēl; **on the left** *ala e-shimēl

left-hand drive drikseeyōn *ala e-shimēl

left-handed ashwel

left luggage office maktab amanēt

leg rigl (f)

legal shar*ɪ

lemon lamoon

lemonade espatis (tm)

lemon tea shay bi lamoon

lend selif; **would you lend me your ...?** mumkin tessalifnee ...?

lens (of camera) *adessa; **contact lenses** *adessēt laska; **I've lost one of my contact lenses** el *adessa da*ɪt minee

lens cap ghata *adessa

Lent e-soom el kebeer

less a'al; **less than an hour** a'al min sa*a; **less than that** a'al min kedda; **less expensive** arkhuhs

lesson dars; **do you give lessons?** inta biteddee diroos?

let: would you let me use it? mumkin tekhaleenee asta*milloo?; **will you let me know?** mumkin te*arafnee?; **I'll let you know** Hab' a'ōlak; **let me try** khaleenee aHawil; **let me go!** sibnamshee!; **let's leave now** yalla nimshee; **let's not go yet** khaleena shwɪya; **will you let me off at ...?** mumkin tenazilnee *and ...?; **apartments to let** sha'a mafroosha lil eegar

letter (in mail) gawab; (of alphabet) Harf; **are there any letters for me?** fee ay gawabaat laya?

letterbox sandoo' el busta

lettuce khass

level crossing mazla'ān

lever (noun) *atala

liable (responsible) mas'ool

liberated: a liberated woman sit Horra

library maktaba

Libya libya

Libyan (man, adjective) leebee; (woman) leebaya

licence, license rokhsa

license plate (on car) nimrit el *arabaya

lid ghata

lie (*untruth*) kizb; **can he lie down for a while?** mumkin hoowa yor'ud shwīya lowsamaнt?; **I want to go and lie down** ana *a-ıyiz arīaн shwīya

lie-in: I'm going to have a lie-in tomorrow ana нагіaн fi sireer bukra

life *omr; **not on your life!** da low нatta *ala *omruhk!; **that's life!** e-donya kedda!

lifebelt tō' nageh

lifeboat markib inkaaz

lifeguard нāris e-shaat

life insurance ta'meen *alel нıa

life jacket sutrit inkaaz

lift (*in hotel etc*) asuhnsayar; **could you give me a lift?** mumkin toowasuhlnee bil *arabaya?; **do you want a lift?** *a-ıyiznee awasuhluhk?; **thanks for the lift** shukran; **a friend gave me a lift** saнibee wosuhlnee

light (*noun*) noor; (*not heavy*) khafeef; **the light was on** e-noor kan welya*; **do you have a light?** (*for cigarette*) ma*ak kabreet?; **a light meal** akla khafeefa; **light blue** azra' fateн

light bulb lamba

lighter (*cigarette*) wala*a

lighter/lightest (*in weight*) akhaf

lighthouse fanar

light meter mi'yes fatнet el *adessa

lightning ra*d

like: I'd like a ... ana *a-ıyiz ...; **I'd like to ...** ana *a-ıyiz ...; **would you like a ...?** inta *a-ıyiz ...?; **would you like to come too?** leek mazeg teegee?; **I'd like to** atmanna; **I like it** baнebboo; **I like you** ana baнebbak; **I don't like it** mabaнebboosh; **he doesn't like it** hoowa mabeнebboosh; **do you like ...?** inta bitнebb ...?; **I like swimming** ana baнebb e-sibaнa; **OK, if you like** OK low teнebb; **what's it like?** zay ay?; **do it like this** kedda; **one like that** waaнid zay da

lime cordial, lime juice *aseer lamoon

line (*on paper*) satr; (*telephone*) khat;

(*of people*) taboor; **would you give me a line?** (*telephone*) mumkin tedeenee khat?

linen (*for beds*) bıyaadaat

linguist *alim bil loghēt; **I'm no linguist** ana mush kwıyis fil loghēt

lining bitaana

lion assad

lip shifa

lip brush forshit roosн

lip gloss 'gloss'

lip pencil alam shefayf

lip salve zebda kakow

lipstick alam roosн

liqueur sharab mo'atuhr

liquor koнol

list lista

listen: I'd like to listen to ... ana *a-ıyiz astimma* lee ...; **listen!** esma*!

liter, litre litr; *see page 118*

litter (*rubbish*) zibella

little sooghıar; **just a little, thanks** shwīya sooghıara; **just a very little** shwīya sooghıyara awee; **a little cream** kreem mush keteer; **a little more** shwīya kamēn; **a little better** aнsen shwīya; **that's too little** (*not enough*) da mush kifaya

live sekin; **I live in ...** ana sekin fee ...; **where do you live?** inta sekin fayn?; **where does he live?** hoowa sekin fayn?; **we live together** eнna sekneen ma*aba*d

lively (*person, town*) nasheet

liver (*in body*) kibd; (*food*) kibda

lizard seнlaya

loaf *ı-esh

lobby (*of hotel*) madkhal

lobster gambaree kebeer

local: local restaurant mat*am baladee; **local cheese** gibna baladee

lock (*noun*) ifl; **it's locked** ma'fool; **I locked myself out of my room** a' el bab et'afel wanna barra

locker (*for luggage etc*) amanēt

log I slept like a log ana nimt zay el mıyit

lollipop muhsaasa; (*ice lolly*) lollee-uhb

London 'london'

lonely waaнeed; **are you lonely?** inta waaнeed?

long taweel; **how long does it take?** bitekhud ad ay?; **is it a long way?** hoowa ba*yeed awee; **a long time** wa't tooweel; **I won't be long** mush нatakhuhr; **don't be long** matitakharsh; **that was long ago** da kan zamān; **I'd like to stay longer** ana *a-ıyiz a*d aktuhr; **long time no see!** mashooftaksh min zamān!; **so long!** ma*asalemma!

long distance call mokalmuh kharigaya

longer/longest atwuhl

loo: where's the loo? fayn el tawalet?; **I want to go to the loo** ana *a-ıyiz arooн li tawalet

look: that looks good da shaklō нelw; **you look tired** shaklak ta*ban; **I'm just looking, thanks** ana batfarag bas shukran; **you don't look your age** (to a man) inta shaklak sooghıyar; (to a woman) intee shaklik sooghıyar; **look at him** busilloo!; **I'm looking for ...** ana badowar *ala ...; **look out!** нasib!; **can I have a look?** mumkin abus?; **can I have a look around?** mumkin etfarag?

loose (button, handle etc) sayib

loose change fakka

lorry looree

lorry driver sawē' looree

lose khesir; **I've lost my ...** ana dıa*t ...; **I'm lost** ana tay-yeh

lost property office, lost and found maktab amanēt

lot: a lot, lots keteer; **not a lot** mush keteer; **a lot of money** feloos keteera; **a lot of women** sittet keteer; **a lot cooler** mitaaree; **I like it a lot** baнebboo keteer; **is it a lot further?** hoowa ba*yeed awee?; **I'll take the (whole) lot** нakhud-hum kuloohum

lotion lōshan

loud *alee; **the music is rather loud** el mooseeka *alee-a awee

lounge (in house, hotel) saala

lousy (meal, hotel, holiday, weather) mush kwıyis

love: I love you (to a man) baнebbak; (to a woman) baнebbik; **he's fallen in love** hoowa beeнebb; **I love Egypt** ana baнebb masr

lovely (meal, view, weather, present etc) gameel

low (prices) rekhees; (bridge) waatee

low beam e-noor el *adee

lower/lowest (prices) arkhus

LP istoo-waana

luck нuz; **hard luck!** 'hard luck'!; **good luck!** нuz sa*yeed!; **just my luck!** da bakhtee!; **it was pure luck** da kan нuz

lucky: that's lucky! da нuz!

lucky charm нegab

luggage shōnuht

lumbago 'lumbago'

lump (medical) waram

lunch gheda

lungs ri'atayn

luxurious (hotel, furnishings) moreeн giddan

luxury *ız

M

mad magnoon
madam madam
magazine migalla
magnificent (*view, day, meal*) momtaz
maid khadamit el ghoruhf
mail (*noun*) bareed; **is there any mail for me?** fee bareed laya?; **where can I mail this?** fayn sandoo' el busta?
mailbox sandoo' el busta
main ra'eesee; **where's the main post office?** fayn maktab el busta e-ra'eesee?
main road (*in town, in country*) e-taree' e-ra'eesee
maize dora
make *amil; **do you make them yourself?** bite*amilhum bee nafsak?; **it's very well made** da ma*mool kwIyis awee; **what does that make altogether?** kuloo bikam?; **I make it only 5 pounds** ana Hassabtoohum khamsa ginay
make-up mikyaasH
make-up remover moozeel lil mikyaasH
malaria malaree-a
male chauvinist pig anzooH
man raagil
manager mōdeer; **may I see the manager?** mumkin ashoof el mōdeer?
mango manga
manicure monōkeer
many keteer
map: a map of ... khareetit ...; **it's not on this map** mush fil khareeta dee
marble (*noun*) rōkhēm
March mēris
marijuana Hasheesh
mark: there's a mark on it *alee

*alēma; **could you mark it on the map for me?** mumkin te*alimoo *alel khareeta?
market (*noun*) soo'
marmalade 'marmalade'
married: are you married? (*to man*) inta mitgowz?; (*to woman*) intee mitgawizza?; **I'm married** ana mitgowz/mitgawizza
mascara 'mascara'
mast saaree
masterpiece toHfa
matches kabreet
material (*cloth*) omāsh; **what is this material?** el omāsh da ay?
matter: it doesn't matter ma*alesh; **what's the matter?** fee ay?
mattress martabba
Mauritania moritanya
Mauritanian (*man, adjective*) moritānee; (*woman*) moritanaya
maximum (*noun*) a*la Had
May mayoo
may: may I have another coffee please? mumkin ahwa tania lowsamaHt?; **may I?** mumkin?
maybe yimkin; **maybe not** yimkin la'
mayonnaise 'mayonnaise'
me: come with me ta*ala ma*ya; **it's for me** da *alashēnee; **it's me** ana; **me too** wana kamēn; *see page 106*
meal: that was an excellent meal el akla kanit momtaza; **does that include meals?** el akl maHsoob?
mean: what does this word mean? e-kelma dee ma*nēha ay?; **what does he mean?** hoowa uhzdoo ay?
measles el Hazba; **German measles** el Hazba el almanaya
measurements ma'assēt
meat laHma

Mecca makkuh; **towards Mecca** tigah makkuh

mechanic: do you have a mechanic here? fee mikaneekee hena?; **do you know where I can find a good mechanic?** inta te*ruhf mekaneekee kwɪyis?

medicine dowa (m)

medieval fil oroon el wusta

Mediterranean el baнr el mōtawassit

medium (adjective) mōtawassit

medium-sized mōtawassit

meet: pleased to meet you tasharuhfna; **where shall we meet?** nit'ābil fayn?; **let's meet up again** khaleena nit'ābil tanee

meeting egtima*

meeting place makkān egtima*

melon shamēma

member *odw; **I'd like to become a member** *a-ɪyiz ab'a *odw

mend: can you mend this? mumkin tisalaн da?

men's room tawalet

mention: don't mention it el *afw

menu kɪma; **may I have the menu please?** mumkin el kɪma lowsamaнt?

merchant tāgir

mess: it's a mess dee hargalla

message: are there any messages for me? fee akhbar *alashenee?; **I'd like to leave a message for ...** *a-ɪyiz aseeb khabar lil ...

metal (noun) ma*adan

metre, meter mitr; see page 117

midday: at midday e-dohr

middle: in the middle fi nus; **in the middle of the road** fi nus e-taree'

midnight: at midnight fi nus el layl

might: I might want to stay another 3 days ana gayz a*ad talat teeyem; **you might have warned me!** kunt *aruhftinee!

migraine suda* shedeed

mild (taste) mush нāmee; (weather) lateef

mile meel; **that's miles away!** da ba*yeed awee!; see page 117

military (adjective) нarbee

milk laban

millimetre, millimeter 'millimetre'

minaret ma'zanna

minced meat laнma mafrooma

mind: I don't mind ma*andeesh mane*a; **would you mind if I ...?** *andak mane*a low ana ...?; **never mind** ma*alesh; **I've changed my mind** ghɪyart ra'ee

mine: it's mine da bita*ee; see page 108

mineral water mɪya ma*adanaya

minimum (adjective) a'al

mint (sweet) ne*ana*

minus naa'is; **minus 3 degrees** talat daragaat taнt e-sifr

minute di'ee'a; **in a minute** kamen shwɪya; **just a minute** estanna shwɪya

mirror miraya

Miss anissa

miss: I miss you bitooнashnee; **there's a ... missing** fee ... naa'is; **we missed the bus** el ōtōbees fatna

mist shaboora

mistake ghalta; **I think there's a mistake here** azon fee ghalta hena

misunderstanding soo' tafēhum

mixture khaaleet

mix-up: there's been some sort of mix-up with ... kan fee soo' tafēhum ma*a ...

modern нadees

modern art fan нadees

moisturizer 'cream'

moment: I won't be a moment mush нatakhuhr

monastery dēr

Monday yum el itneen

money feloos (f); **I don't have any money** ma*eesh feloos; **do you take English/American money?** bitekhud istuhrleenee/dollaraat?

month shahr

monument tizkaar

moon uhmuhr

moorings marsa

moped biskilitta

more tanee; **may I have some more?**
mumkin tanee?; **more coffee, please**
ahwa tania lowsamaHt; **no more,
thanks** da kifaya shukran; **more
expensive** aghla; **more than 50**
aktar min khamseen; **more than that**
aktar min kedda; **a lot more** aktar; **I
don't stay there any more** ana mush
sēkkin hinak
morning subH; **good morning** sabaH
el kheer; **this morning** e-naharda e-
subH; **in the morning** e-subH
Morocco el maghrib
Moroccan maghribee
moslem muslim
mosque gāmi*a
mosquito namoosa
mosquito net shabakit namoos
most: I like this one most ana
bafuhduhl da; **most of the time**
mo*zuhm el wa't; **most hotels**
mo*zuhm el fanādi'
mother um; **my mother** ummee
mother of pearl saduhf
motif (*in pattern*) zaghraffa
motor mator
motorbike mōtōsikl
motorboat luhnsh
motorist sawē'
motor yacht yakht
mountain gabbal; **up in the
mountains** fil gabbal; **a mountain
village** kaaria fil gabbal
mouse far
moustache shanab
mouth bo'
move: he's moved to another hotel
hoowa na'al li fondō' tanee; **could
you move your car?** mumkin tin'il
*arabeeyetuhk?

movie film; **let's go to the movies**
yalla nerooH e-sinima
movie camera kamira sinima-aya
movie theater 'cinema'
moving: a very moving tune
naghama tera'as
Mr ōstez
Mrs madam
Ms *no equivalent*
much keteer; **much better** aHsen
keteer; **much cooler** abruhd; **not
much** mush keteer; **not so much**
mush keteer
muezzin mo'azin
muffler (*car*) *albit e-shakmān
mug: I've been mugged ana etsar'at
muggy: it's very muggy e-rotooba
*alia awee
mule gaHsh
mummy (*in tomb*) momee-a
mumps eltihab fil gōdad
murals (*paintings*) risoom milawina;
(*hieroglyphics*) ni'oosh milawina
muscle *adala
museum matHaf
music museeka; **kanoon music**
museekat anoon; **do you have the
sheet music for ...?** *andak e-nōta el
musikaya lil ...?
musician musikaar
mussels om el khilool
must: I must ... ana lezim ...; **I
mustn't drink ...** ana mamnoo-a*
min shorb ...; **you mustn't forget**
matinsesh
mustache shanab
my: my room ōtee; **my ticket**
tazkatee; *see page 105*
myself: I'll do it myself Ha*amiloo bi
nafsee

N

nail (*of finger*) dofr; (*in wood*) musmar
nail clippers asaafit dowaafir
nailfile mabruhd dowaafir
nail polish milamma* lil dowaafir
nail polish remover tenir
nail scissors ma'as dowaafir
naked *ɪree-ēn
name ism; **what's your name?** ismak
ay?; **what's its name?** ismhoo ay?;
my name is ... ismee ...
nap: he's having a nap hoowa
biyēkhud ghefwit num
napkin (*serviette*) foota
nappy kafoola
nappy-liners *azl nabee
narrow (*road*) day-yeh'
nasty (*taste, person, weather, cut*) fazee-
a*
national dowlee
nationality ginsaya
natural tabee*ɪyee
naturally (*of course*) tab*an; (*in a
natural way*) bi taba*
nature (*trees etc*) tabee*a
nausea bi suda*
nauseous: I'm feeling nauseous ana
ʜassis bi suda*
near gamb; **is it near here?** hoowa
orɪyib min hena?; **near the window**
gamb e-shebek; **do you go near ...?**
inta bit*adee *ala ...?; **where is the
nearest ...?** fayn a'rab ...?
nearby orɪyib awee
nearly ta'reeban
nearside wheel el *agala el orɪyibba
neat (*room etc*) uhneek; (*drink*) lee
waʜdo
necessary darooree; **is it necessary
to ...?** hoowa darooree lee ...?; **it's
not necessary** mush darooree
neck (*of body*) ra'ba; (*of dress, shirt*)

ye'ah
necklace *a'od
necktie garafatta
need: I need a ... ana meʜtag ...; **do
I need a ...?** aʜtag ...?; **it needs
more salt** meʜtag shwɪyit malʜa;
there's no need maloosh lezoom;
there's no need to shout! maloosh
lezoom teeza*a'!
needle ibra
negative (*film*) *afreet
neighbo(u)r gar
neighbo(u)rhood geera
neither: neither of us wala waaʜid
minna; **neither one (of them)** wala
waaʜid fee hum; **neither ... nor ...**
la ... wala ...; **neither do I** walana;
neither does he wala hoowa
nephew (*brother's son*) ibn akh; (*sister's
son*) ibn okht
nervous *asabee
net (*fishing, tennis*) shabakuh
neurotic ekhteelal el a*saab
neutral (*gear*) filmoor
never abadan
new gedeed; **new moon** hilāl
news akhbar (*f*); **is there any news?**
fee ay akhbar?
newspaper gurnaan; **do you have
any English newspapers?** *andak ay
gurɪyid ingileezee?
newsstand bɪya* gurɪyid
New Year e-sana e-gedeeda; **Happy
New Year** *a-am gedeed sa*yeed
New Year's Eve laylit raas e-sana
New York 'new york'
New Zealand nyoozlanda
New Zealander (*man*) nyoozlandee;
(*woman*) nyoozlandaya
next: the next one ellee ba*dō; **it's at
the next corner** *and e-nassia ellee

gaya; **next week** el isbooa* e-gay;
next Monday litneen e-gay; **next to
the post office** gamb el busta; **the
one next to that** el waaHid ellee
gamb da
nextdoor (*adverb, adjective*) el bayt
ellee gambenna
next of kin areeb
nice (*person, meal, town, day*) kwIyis;
that's very nice of you da zo'
minak; **a nice cold drink** mashroob
se'a* awee
nicer/nicest aHla
nickname ism e-dalla*
niece (*brother's daughter*) bint akh;
(*sister's daughter*) bint okht
night layl; **for one night** lee mōdit
layla waHda; **for three nights** lee
mōdit talaat layalee; **good night**
tisbaH *ala kheer; **at night** bil layl
nightclub malha laylee (*m*)
nightdress amees num
night flight reHla laylayla
nightie amees num
night-life HIyat e-layl
nightmare kaboos
night porter ghefeer
Nile nahr e-neel
nits (*bugs, in hair*) aml
no la'; **I've no money** ma*I-eesh
feloos; **there's no more** mafeesh; **no
more than ...** mush aktar min ...; **oh
no!** (*upset*) akh!
nobody mafeesh Had, wala waaHid
noise dowsha
noisy *amil dowsha; **it's too noisy** da
dowsha awee
nomad badawee
non-alcoholic min gheer koHol;
non-alcoholic drink mashroobaat
gheer kaHolaya
none wala Haga, mafeesh; **none of
them** wala waaHid fee hum
nonsense kalēm fērigh

non-smoking (*compartment, section of
plane*) mamnoo*a e-tadkheen
non-stop (*travel*) *alatool
no-one mafeesh Had, wala waaHid
nor: nor do I walana; **nor does he**
wala hoowa
normal *adee
north shimēl; **to the north** li shimēl
northeast e-shimēl e-shar'ee; **to the
northeast** li shimēl e-shar'ee
Northern Ireland irlanda e-
shamalaya
northwest e-shimēl el ghaarbee; **to
the northwest** li shimēl el ghaarbee
Norway norweeg
nose marakheen; **my nose is bleeding**
marakheenee bitgeeb dam
not mush; **I don't smoke**
mabadakhansh; **he didn't say anything** hoowa ma'elsh aya Haga; **it's
not important** mush mōhim; **not
that one** mush da; **not for me** mush
*alashēnee; *see page 112*
note (*bank note*) wara'; (*written message
etc*) moozakerra
notebook nōta
nothing mafeesh Haga, wala Haga
November novimbuhr
now delwa'tee; **not now** mush
delwa'tee
nowhere wala Hetta
nuisance: he's being a nuisance
(*pestering woman etc*) hoowa mida-
y'inee
numb (*limb etc*) minamil
number (*figure*) nimra; **what number?**
nimra kam?
number plates nimer el *arabaya
nurse momaredduh
nursery (*at airport etc, for children*)
Hadaana
nut gōz; (*for bolt*) samoola
nutter: he's a nutter (*is crazy*) hoowa
magnoon

O

oar migdaf

oasis waнa; **at the oasis** fil waнa

obelisk misella

obligatory igbāree

oblige: much obliged (*thank you*) shukran

obnoxious (*person*) fazee-a*

obstetrician akhissaa'ee uhmraad el wilāda

obvious: that's obvious da waadeн

occasionally aнeeyēnan

o'clock e-sa*a; *see page 116*

October oktōbuhr

octopus akhtaboot

odd (*strange*) ghereeb; (*number*) fardee

odometer *adad el masafēt

of: the name of the hotel ism el fondō'; **the owner of the car** saaнeb el *arabaya; **the price of the tickets** taman e-tazkara; **have one of mine** khud waaнid min bita*ee; *see page 108*

off: 20% off takhfeed *ashreen fil maya; **the lights were off** e-noor kan matfee; **just off the main road** taнweeda waнda min e-tahree' el *amoomee

offend: don't be offended matiz*alsh

office (*place of work*) maktab

officer (*said to policeman*) effendim

official (*noun*) mas'ool; **is that official?** da rasmee?

off-season mush fil moosim

off-side wheel el *agala el bay*yeeda

often dıman; **not often** aнyennan

oil (*for car, for salad*) zayt; (*crude oil*) bitrōl; **it's losing oil** bitsarab zayt; **will you change the oil?** mumkin teghıyar e-zayt?; **the oil light's flashing** kashef e-zayt baynowar

oil fields нokool el bitrōl

oil painting rasma alwān bi zayt

oil pressure daght e-zayt

oil rigs ag-hizza listikhraag el bitrōl

oil tanker (*ship*) na'lit bitrōl

oil well aabaar bitrōl

ointment marhuhm

OK 'ok'; **are you OK?** inta kwıyis?; **that's OK thanks** da tamem, shukran; **that's OK by me** ana mowafi'

old (*thing*) adeem; (*person*) *agooz; **how old are you?** *andak kam sana?

old age pensioner kebeer fi sin

old-fashioned mōda adeema

old town (*old part of town*) ... el adeema; **Old Cairo** masr el'adeema

olive zetoon

olive oil zayt zetoon

Oman *amān

Omani (*man, adjective*) *amānee; (*woman*) *amanaya

omelet(t)e omlit

on *ala; **on the roof** *ala suht-н; **on the beach** *alel bilasн; **on Friday** yum el gom*a; **on television** fi teleeviyōn; **I don't have it on me** mush ma*aya; **this drink's on me** el mashroob da *alaya; **a book on Cairo** kitab *an el kaнeera; **the warning light comes on** noor e-teeнzeer beenawar; **the light was on** e-noor kan wēle*a; **what's on in town?** fee ay fil balad?; **it's just not on!** (*not acceptable*) da mayınfa*sh

once (*one time*) mara waнda; **at once** (*immediately*) delwa'tee

one waaнid; (*for feminine nouns*) waнda; **that one** da; **the green one** el waaнid el akhdar; **the one with the black skirt on** el waнda ellee

labsa goonilla sōdaa; **the one in the blue shirt** el waaнid ellee labis amees azra'
onion basal
only bas; **only one** waaнid bas; **only once** mara waнda bas; **it's only 9 o'clock** e-sa*a tissa* bas; **I've only just arrived** ana lessa waasil
open (*adjective*) fateн; **when do you open?** biteftaн emta?; **in the open** (*in open air*) fil khala; **it won't open** mush *a-ıyiz yitfeteн
opening times mowa*ıd el *amel
open top (*car*) makshoof
opera obra
operation (*medical*) *amilaya
operator (*telephone*) *amil e-telefōnet, e-switsh
opportunity forsa
opposite: opposite the mosque ōdam e-gāmi*a; **it's directly opposite** ōdam bizobt
oppressive (*heat*) (*colloquial word*) shedeeda; (*formal word*) sa*ab el eнtimel
optician akhisaa'ee nuhdaaraat
optimistic mutafe'il
optional ekhtee-yeree
or ow
orange (*fruit*) bortoo'an; (*colour*) bortoo'aanee
orange juice (*fresh*) *aseer bortoo'an taaza; (*fizzy, diluted*) *aseer bortoo'an
orchestra 'orchestra'
order: could we order now? (*in restaurant*) mumkin nutlub delwa'tee?; **I've already ordered** ana talubt khaalas; **I didn't order that** ana matalubtish da; **it's out of order** (*lift etc*) mush shaghēl
ordinary *adee
organization (*company*) shirka
organize nuhzuhm; **could you organize it?** mumkin tenuhzuhmoo?
original aslee; **is it an original?** da aslee?
ornament zeena
ostentatious (*clothes, colour etc*) mifakhfakh

other tanee; **the other waiter** el garsōn e-tanee; **the other one** el waahid e-tanee; **are there any others?** fee tanee?; **some other time, thanks** wa'at tanee, shukran
otherwise wa illa
ouch! ıyee!
ought: he ought to be here soon hoowa mafrood yeekoon hena ba*d shwıya
ounce *see page 118*
our: our home baytna; **our suitcases** shōnuhtna; **to our hotel** lil fondō; *see page 105*
ours bita*anna; **that's ours** da bita*anna; *see page 108*
out: he's out hoowa bara; **get out!** okhrug bara!; **I'm out of money** ma*ı-eesh feloos; **a few kilometres out of town** bara el balad shwıya
outboard (motor) mator
outdoors bara
outlet (*electrical*) bareeza
outside bara; **can we sit outside?** mumkin no'a*od bara?
outskirts: on the outskirts of ... fee dawaнee ...
oven forn
over: over here hena; **over there** hinak; **over 100** fo' el maya; **I'm burnt all over** ana etнarra't min e-shams; **the holiday's over** el agēzza khalsit
overcharge: you've overcharged me inta khat feloos keteer
overcoat baltoo
overcooked mistiwee awee
overexposed (*photograph*) minnawarra
overheat: it's overheating (*car*) el mator beeyeskhan
overland (*travel*) bi taree'
overlook: overlooking the sea yootul *ala el baнr
overnight (*travel*) tool e-layl
oversleep: I overslept ana etakhart fi num
overtake *ada
overweight (*person*) fo' el wazn
owe: how much do I owe you? ana

*alaya kam?
own: my own ... ...-ee; my own
house baytee; my own daughter
bintee; my own money feloosee;
are you on your own? inta lee

waHdak?; I'm on my own ana lee
waHdee
owner (colloquial word) saaHib; (more
formal word) mālik
oyster maHarr

P

pack: a pack of cigarettes *albit
saggayar; I'll go and pack ana
HarooH asta*id
package (at post office) tard
package holiday reHla shamla
package tour reHla shamla
packed out: the place was packed
out el makkan kan zaHma awee
packet *albuh; a packet of cigarettes
*albit saggayar
paddle (noun) migdaf
padlock (noun) ifl
page (of book) suhf-Huh; could you
page Mr ...? mumkin tinādee el
ōstez ...?
pain waga*; I have a pain here
andee waga hena
painful mo'lim
painkillers musakin
paint (oil paint) lōn zayt; (water colours)
alwān mIya; (on car) dihan; I'm
going to do some painting (artist)
ana rIaH arsim
paintbrush (artist's) forshit alwān
painting soora
pair: a pair of ... itneen min ...
pajamas bisHaama
Pakistan bakistan
Pakistani (man, adjective) bakistānee;
(woman) bakistanaya
pal saaHib
palace asr
pale (face) misfuhr; (colour) fateH;
pale blue azra' fateH
Palestine falasteen
Palestinian (man, adjective)

falasteenee; (woman) falasteenaya
palm tree nakhla
palpitations nuhbd
pancake feteera
panic: don't panic matit-re*absh
panties kulot Hareemee
pants (trousers) bantalōn; (underpants)
kulot
panty girdle korsay
pantyhose sharab filay
paper wara'; (newspaper) gurnaan; a
piece of paper Hettit wara'
paper handkerchiefs manadeel wara'
papyrus wara' el baardee
paraffin barafeen
parallel: parallel to ... moo-wazee lee
...
parasol shamsaya Hareemee
parcel tard
parched (land, person) gaf
pardon (me)? (didn't understand)
na*m?
parents: my parents waldee wee
walditee
park (noun) mow'af; where can I
park? arkin fayn?; there's nowhere
to park mafeesh makkān arkin fee
parking lights e-noor el waatee
parking lot mō'af *arabeeyaat
parking place: there's a parking
place! fee makkān terkin fee!
part (noun) guz'
partner (boyfriend) saHibee; (girlfriend)
saHbitee; (in business) shireek
party (group) magmoo*a; (celebration)
Hafla; let's have a party yalla

ne*amil Hafla

pass (*in mountains*) momarr; (*verb: overtake*) saba'; **he passed out** oghma *alay; **he made a pass at me** hoowa Hawil ma*aya

passable (*road*) saaleH li sawē'a

passenger rēkib

passport bassbort

past: in the past fil maadee; **just past the bank** ba*d el bank; **half past two** itneen wi nus; *see page 116*

pastry (*dough*) *ageena; (*small cake*) feteera

patch: could you put a patch on this? mumkin tekhı-uht da?

path momarr

patient: be patient osborr

patio varanduh

pattern batrōn; **a dress pattern** batrōn; **I like the pattern on that ...** baHebb e-tuhsmeem ellee *alal ...

paunch kirsh

pavement (*sidewalk*) raseef

pay (*verb*) dafa*; **can I pay, please?** mumkin adfa* lowsamaHt?; **it's already paid for** el Hisab khaalis; **I'll pay for this** Hadfa* lee da

pay phone telefōn *amoomee

peace salam

peace and quiet heedoo'

peach khōkhaa

peanuts fool sudānee

pear komitra

pearl loolee

peas bisilla

peasant fellaH

peculiar (*taste, custom*) ghereeb

pedal (*in car*) dawāsa; (*on bike*) beedal

pedestrian mushēh

pedestrian crossing *aboor mushēh

pedestrian precinct lil mushēh faakuht

pedicure 'pedicure'

pee: I need to go for a pee lezim arooH li tawalet

peg (*for washing*) masHbak; (*for tent*) wattad

pen alam; **do you have a pen?** ma*ak alam?

pencil alam roosaas

penfriend saadee' morasla; **shall we be penfriends?** mumkin nitrēssil?

penicillin bensilleen

penknife matoowa

pen pal saadee' morasla

pensioner *agooz

people nās; **a lot of people** nās keteer; **the Egyptian people** el masrayeen

pepper (*spice*) filfil eswid; **green pepper** filfil akhdar; **red pepper** filfil aHmar

peppermint (*sweet*) nea*na*

per: per night fil layla; **how much per hour?** beekam e-sa*a?

per cent fil maya

perfect tamem

perfume reeHa

perhaps gayz

period (*of time*) mōda; (*menstruation*) el *aada

perm kanteesh

permit (*noun*) tuhsreeH

Persian Gulf el khaleeg el farisee

person shaakhs

pessimistic mutashē'im

petrol benzeen

petrol can suhfeeHet benzeen

petrol station maHattit benzeen

petrol tank (*in car*) 'tank'

petrol tanker (*truck*) *arabayit na'l benzeen

pharmacy agzakhēnna

Pharaoh far*ōn

phone *see* **telephone**

photogenic: she is very photogenic haya Helwa awee fi siwuhr

photograph (*noun*) soora; **would you take a photograph of us?** mumkin tessawurna?

photographer mussawaraatee

phrase: a useful phrase gomla mufeeda

phrasebook daleel seeyaHee

pianist *azif beeyanō

piano beeyanō

piastre uhrsh

pickpocket nashēl

pick up: when can I pick them up? (*clothes from laundry etc*) emta āgee akhudhum?; **will you come and pick me up?** mumkin teegee tekhudnee?
picnic (*noun*) nōzha
picture soora
piece нetta; **a piece of ...** нettit ...
pig khanzeer
pigeon нamāma
piles (*medical*) el bawaseer
pile-up (*crash*) нadsa
pilgrim нag
pilgrimage нeg; **have you made a pilgrimage to Mecca yet?** inta нagit?
pill нabba; **I'm on the pill** ana bēkhud нeboob manna* el нaml
pillar *amood
pillarbox sandoo' busta
pillow makhadda
pillow case kees makhadda
pin (*noun*) daboos
pineapple ananas
pineapple juice *aseer ananas
pink bamba
pint *see page 119*
pipe (*for smoking*) beeba; (*for water*) masoora
pipe cleaner monuнzif beeba
pipeline anabeeb bitrōl
pipe tobacco dokhēn beeba
pity: it's a pity ma*alesh
pizza beetza
place (*noun*) makkān; **is this place taken?** нad a*ıd hena?; **would you keep my place for me?** mumkin tekhelee bālak min makēnee?; **at my place** fee baytee; **at your place** fee baytak
plain (*food*) *adee; (*not patterned*) sēda
plane tıyara
plant nabat
plaster cast ālib gibs
plastic blastik
plastic bag shanta blastik
plate taba'
platform raseef; **which platform, please?** raseef nimra kam

lowsamaнt?
play (*verb*) le*ıb; (*noun: in theatre*) muhsraнaya
playboy blay boy
playground malla*b
pleasant sar
please lowsamaнt; **yes please** ıwa lowsamaнt; **could you please ...?** mumkin ... lowsamaнt?
plenty: plenty of ... keteer min ...; **that's plenty, thanks** da kifaya shukran
pleurisy eltihab el bilyora
pliers zaradaya
plonk (*wine*) nebeet; (*cheap wine*) nebeet rekhees
plug (*electrical*) feesha; (*for car*) tuhbit el kartēr; (*in sink*) suhdēdit нōd
plughole *ın el нōd
plum bar'oo'a
plumber sabēk
plus (*arithmetic*) zē'id
p.m. ba*d e-dohr; **at 2.00 p.m.** e-sa*a itneen ba*d e-dohr; **at 10.00 p.m.** e-sa*a *ashara bil layl
pneumonia eltihab e-re'a
pocket gib; **in my pocket** fee geebee
pocketbook (*woman's handbag*) shantit eed
pocketknife matwa
point: could you point to it? mumkin teshēwer *allay?; **four point six** arba* wi sitta min *ashara; **there's no point** mafeesh fıda
points (*in car*) ablateen
poison sim
poisonous musamim
police bolees; **call the police!** etessil bil bolees!
policeman *askaree; (*higher rank, with stars*) zaabit
police station esm e-shorta
polish (*noun*) warneesh; **will you polish my shoes?** mumkin telama* gazmitee?
polite mo'adab
politician seeyēsee
politics *a-elm e-seeyēssa
polluted millawis

pomegranate romaana
pond birka
pony see-see
pool (for swimming) Hammem sibaHa; (game) billeeyardō
poor (not rich) fē'eer; (quality) mush kwIyis; **poor old Mohamed!** ye*Inee *ala moHammad!
Pope el baabaa
pop music mooseeka gharbaya; (western) mooseeka afrangee
popsicle (tm) lollee-uhb
pop singer mōghānee
popular maHboob
population e-sha*ab
port (for boats) meena; (drink) bōrt
porter (in hotel, at station) shIyel
portrait soora
Portugal bortooghel
poser: he is a poser hoowa shayif nafsoo
posh (restaurant) fēkhir giddan; (people) fo'awee
possibility eHtimal
possible: is it possible to ...? mumkin ...?; **as ... as possible** bee ... mIyumkim
post (noun: mail) busta; **could you post this for me?** mumkin termee el gawab da fil busta?
postbox sandoo' busta
postcard kart
poster (advertisement) ē*alēn; (as souvenir) soora
poste restante you have a post box number: sandoo' bareed rakuhm
post office maktab bareed; (colloquial word) el busta
pot (for cooking) edra; (teapot) baraad shay; **a pot of tea for two** shay litneen
potato bataatis (f)
potato chips bataatis maHamarra
potato salad salaatit bataatis
pots and pans (cooking implements) Hellel
pottery (objects) khazaf; (workshop) masna* khazaf
pound (Egyptian money) ginay; (British)

estirleenēe; see page 118
pour: it's pouring down bitnuhtuhr gāmid
powder (for face) budra
powdered milk laban budra
power cut el kaharaba ma'too*a; **there's been a power cut** el kaharaba etatIt
power point bareeza
power station maHattit towleed el kaharaba
practise, practice: I need to practise meHtag tamreen
pram *arabit tefl
prawn cocktail koktayl gambaree
prawns gambaree
prayer salaa
prefer: I prefer ... ana afuhduhl ...
preferably: preferably not tomorrow el aHsen mush bukra
pregnant Hāmil
prescription (for chemist) rooshetta
present (gift) hidaya; **here's a present for you** (to a man) hidaya *alashēnak; (to a woman) hidaya *alashēnik; **at present** delwa'tee
president (of company, country) ra'ees
press: could you press these? mumkin tekwee dōl?
pretty gameel; **it's pretty expensive** da ghēlee awee
price taman
prickly heat Hamooneel
priest assees
prime minister ra'ees el wozuh-ruh
prince ameer
princess ameera
print (noun: picture) soora
printed matter muhtbō*aat
priority (in driving): **it was my priority** da kan taree'ee
prison sig-n
private khaas; **private bath** bi Hammēm
prize gayza
probably gayz
problem mushkilla; **I have a problem** *andee mushkilla; **no problem!** mafeesh mushkilla!

program(me) (*noun*) birnāmig
promise: I promise aw*ıdak; **is that
a promise?** da wa*d?
**pronounce: how do you pronounce
this?** izzay tintuh' da?; **I can't
pronounce it** mush adir a'ooloo
properly kwıyis; **it's not repaired
properly** matsuhllaнsh kwıyis
prophet nabee
prostitute moomis
protect saan
protein remover (*for contact lenses*)
maнlool lituhndeef
Protestant brotistant
proud fakhoor
prunes bar'oo nashif
public (*adjective*) *amoomee
public convenience tawalet
public holiday agēzza rasmaya
pudding нelw
pull shad; **he pulled out without in-
dicating** hoowa tela* min gheer
mıyeddee eshara
pullover bullōvar

pump (*for water*) toolomba; (*for bike*)
minfēkh; (*for car*) howa
punctual: he is punctual hoowa
moнaafiz *ala el mo-a*ıd
puncture (*noun*) khorm
pure (*silk etc*) saafee
pure orange juice bortoo'aan khaalis
purple banafsigee
purse (*for money*) kees; (*handbag*)
shanta
push za'; **don't push in!** matzo'ish
push-chair *arabit tefl
put нott; **where did you put ...?** inta
нattit fayn ...?; **where can I put ...?**
aнott ... fayn?; **could you put the
lights on?** mumkin too-ala* e-noor?;
will you put the light out? mumkin
tetfee e-noor?; **you've put the price
up** inta *alayt e-sa*r; **could you put
us up for the night?** mumkin
naynām hena elleelādee?
pyjamas bisнaama
pyramid haram; **the Pyramids** el
ahramaat

Q

Qatar kuнtuhr
Qatari min kuнtuhr
quality nōwa; **poor quality** nōwa*
mush kwıyis; **good quality** nōwa
kwıyis
quarantine нaguhr seнee
quart *see page 119*
quarter rub'a*; **quarter of an hour**
rub'a* sa*a; *see page 116*
quay marsa
quayside: on the quayside нafit el
marsa
queen malika; (*cards*) bint
question soo'el; **that's out of the**

question da mush mumkin
queue (*noun*) taboor; **there was a big
queue** kan fee taboor taweel
quick saree*; **that was quick** da
saree* awee; **which is the
quickest way?** ay asra* taree'?
quicker/quickest asra*
quickly bisor*a
quiet (*place, hotel*) haddee; **be quiet!**
hidoo' lowsamaнt!
quinine kineen
quite: quite a lot keteer awee; **it's quite
different** da mokhtalif awee; **I'm not
quite sure** ana mush mōta-akid

R

rabbit arnab

rabies da' el kalb

race (*noun: for horses, cars etc*) seebe';
I'll race you there ana Hazba'k
hinak

racket (*sport*) muhdruhb

radiator (*of car, in room*) raydater

radio radyō; **on the radio** *ala radyō

rag (*for cleaning*) kohna

rail: by rail bi sikka el Hadeed

railroad, railway e-sikka el Hadeed

railroad crossing mazla'an

rain (*noun*) nuhtara; **in the rain** fi
nuhtara; **it's raining** bitnuhtuhr

rape (*noun*) eghteesaab

rare (*object etc*) nadir; (*steak*) mush
mistiwee awee

rash (*on skin*) tuhfH

rat far

rate (*for changing money*) se*ar; **what's
the rate for the pound?** ay se*ar el
estuhrleenee?; **what are your rates?**
(*at car hire etc*) as*aruhk ay?

rather: it's rather late dee wakhree
shwIya; **I'd rather ...** ana afuhduhl
...; **I'd rather have rice** ana
afuhduhl ruz

raw (*meat*) nay

razor (*dry, electric*) makanit Hila'a

razor blades amwes Hila'a

reach: within easy reach orIyib

read kara'; **I can't read it** mush a'dar
a'ra; **could you read it out?** mumkin
tea'ra bisōt *alee?; **I want to learn to
read Arabic** ana *a-Iyiz at*allim
*arabee

ready gehiz; **when will it be ready?**
HIkoon gehiz emta?; **I'll go and get
ready** ana rIaH asta*Id; **I'm not
ready yet** ana mush gehiz

real Ha'ee-ee

really awee; **I really must go** ana
lezim amshee; **is it really necessary?**
da darooree awee?

realtor maktab simsar

rear: at the rear fil akhir

rear wheels el *agal el waraanee

rearview mirror mirraya

reasonable (*prices etc*) ma*'ool; **be
reasonable** khaleek ma*'ool

receipt wasl

recently min orIyib

reception (*in hotel*) isti'bel; (*for guests*)
Haflit isti'bel

reception desk el isti'bel

receptionist moowazuhf isti'bel

recipe wasfa; **can you give me the
recipe for this?** mumkin tedeenee el
wasfa?

recognize et*aruhf *al; **I didn't
recognize it** ma*reftoohoosh

**recommend: could you recommend
...?** mumkin te'ōlee ...?

record (*noun: music*) istoowaana

record player bikuhb

red aHmar

Red Sea el baHr el aHmar

red wine nebeet aHmar

reduction (*in price*) takhfeed

reeds gheb

refinery ma*mal takreer bitrōl

refreshing mon*ash

refrigerator talaga

refund targee*; **do I get a refund?**
mumkin araga* da?; **no refund**
mafeesh targee*a

region monte'a

registered: by registereed mail
bareed musagil

registration number nimrit el
*arabaya

relative: my relatives areebee

relaxing: it's very relaxing da mohadee awee
reliable (*person, car*) ameen
religion deen
religious (*person*) mōtadayin
remains (*of old city etc*) kharabaat
remember: I don't remember mush fakir; **I remember** ana fakir; **do you remember?** inta fakir?
remote (*village etc*) ba*yeed
rent (*noun: for apartment etc*) igar; (*verb: car etc*) uhguhr; **I'd like to rent a bike/car** ana a*ıyiz a-uhguhr *agala/*arabaya
rental car *arabaya mituhgara
repair (*verb*) suhllaH; **can you repair it?** mumkin tisalaH da?
repeat karrar; **could you repeat that?** mumkin tekarrar tanee?
representative (*noun: of company*) ne'ib
request (*noun*) tuhluhb
rescue (*verb*) uhnkuhz
reservation Hagz; **I have a reservation** *ana Hagazt hena
reserve Hagaz; **I reserved a room in the name of ...** ana Hagazt ōda bee ism ...; **can I reserve a table for tonight?** mumkin aHgiz tarabayza lil layla dee?
rest (*repose*) raHa; (*remainder*) be'ee; **I need a rest** meHtag istiraHa; **the rest of the group** be'ee el magmoo*a
restaurant mat*am
rest house istiraHa
rest room tawalet
retired: I'm retired ana *alel ma*ash
return: a return to Cairo tazkarit *a-ooda lil kaheera; **I'll return it tomorrow** ana Haraga*ha bukra
returnable: is this returnable? da kaabil lil targee*?
reverse gear marshidayar
revolting mo'rif
rheumatism 'rheumatism'
rib dilla*; **a cracked rib** dilla* maksoor
ribbon (*for hair*) shireet

rice ruz
rich (*person*) ghenee; (*food*) dism; **it's too rich** dism awee
ride: can you give me a ride into town? mumkin te-wasuhlnee lee nus el balad?; **thanks for the ride** shukran
ridiculous: that's ridiculous da ginoon
right (*correct*) saH; (*not left*) yimeen; **you're right** inta *ala Ha'; **you were right** inta kunt *ala Ha'; **that's right** da saH; **that can't be right** da mush saH; **right!** saH!; **is this the right road for ...?** da e-taree' lil ...?; **on the right** *alel yimeen; **turn right** Howid yimeen; **not right now** mush delwa'tee
right-hand drive direkseeyōn *alel yimeen
ring (*in finger*) khetim; **I'll ring you** Haatissil beek
ring road taree' da'ēree
ripe (*fruit*) mistiwee
rip-off: it's a rip-off dee ser'a; **rip-off prices** as*ar khayalaya
risky khuhtuhr; **it's too risky** khuhtuhr awee
river nahr; **by the river** gamb e-nahr
road taree'; **is this the road to ...?** da taree' lil ...?; **further down the road** ōdam shwıya
road accident Hadsa
road hog sawe' magnoon
road map khareetit toro'
roadside: by the roadside *ala gamb e-taree'
roadsign esharit toro'
roadwork(s) tuhsleeH toro'
roast beef rōz beef
rob: I've been robbed anatsara't
robe (*housecoat*) rōb shambuhr
rock (*stone*) Hagguhr; **on the rocks** (*with ice*) bee talg
rocky (*coast etc*) sakhree
roll (*bread*) feeno medowar
Roman rōmānee; **Roman ruins** asaar rōmanaya
Roman Catholic kathōleekee

romance kesit Hobb
roof suht-H; **on the roof** *alel suht-H; **can we sleep on the roof?** mumkin ninam fi suH-t?
roof rack shabakit *arabaya
room ōda; **do you have a room?** *andak ōda?; **a room for two people** ōda litneen; **a room for three nights** ōda lee talateeyem; **a room with a bathroom** ōda bi Hammem; **in my room** fee ōtee; **there's no room** mafeesh maken
room service khedma lil aywad
rope Habl
rose warda
rosé (*wine*) wardee
Rosetta stone Haggar rasheed
rough (*sea*) hayig; (*crossing*) sa*ab; **the engine sounds a bit rough** fee *Iyib fil mator; **I've been sleeping rough** (*in open air*) ana nimt fil khala
roughly (*approximately*) ta'reeban
roulette 'roulette'
round (*adjective*) medowar; **it's my round** da dooree
round-trip: a round-trip ticket to ...

tazkarit *a-ooda lil ...
route taree'; **what's the best route?** ay aHsen taree'?
rowboat, rowing boat markib
rubber (*material*) mataat; (*eraser*) asteeka
rubber band astik
rubbish (*waste*) zibella; (*poor quality goods*) nōwa* mush kwIyis; **that's rubbish!** (*nonsense*) da kalem faadee
rucksack shanta li dahr
rude mush mo'adab; **he was very rude** hoowa kan aleel el adab
rug sigada
ruins kharabaat
rum 'rum'; **rum and coke** 'rum' wa kakōla
run (*person*) geree; **I go running** (*habitually*) ana bagree; **quick, run!** egree bisor*a!; **how often do the buses run?** el ōtōbees beeyetla* kul ad ay?; **he's been run over** hoowa indes; **I've run out of gas/petrol** mafeesh benzeen
rupture (*medical*) fat'
Russia russya

S

saccharine sookaree
sad Hazeen
saddle (*for bike*) korsee; (*for horse*) sirg
safe (*not in danger*) kwIyis; (*not dangerous*) amān; **will it be safe here?** Hatkoon amān hena?; **is it safe to drink?** dee salHa li shorb?; **is it a safe beach for swimming?** da bilasH amān li sibaHa?; **could you put this in your safe?** mumkin tisheel da fee khaznetak?
safety pin daboos masHbak
Sahara saHara
sail (*noun*) shiraa*; **let's go sailing** yalla nerooH 'sailing'

sailboard (*noun*) 'sailboard'
sailboarding: I like sailboarding ana baHebb 'windsurfing'
sailor baHarr
salad salaata
salad cream salaatit kreem
salad dressing salsa li salaata
sale: is it for sale? da lil baya*?; **it's not for sale** mush lil baya*
sales clerk (*male*) baya*; (*female*) baya*a
salmon salamō
salt malH
salty: it's too salty da Hadi' awee
same zay; **one the same as this**

waaHid zay da; **the same again, please** waaHid tanee lowsamaHt; **have a good time — same to you** wa't sa*yeed — wa enta; **it's all the same to me** kuloo zay ba*dō; **thanks all the same** shukran

sand raml

sandals sanduhl; **a pair of sandals** sanduhl

sandstorm *aasifa ramlaya

sandwich 'sandwich'; **a cheese sandwich** 'sandwich' gibnuh; **felafel sandwich** 'sandwich' ta*amaya

sandy ramlee; **a sandy beach** bilasH ramlee

sanitary napkins/towels fewot saHaya

sarcastic mohazza'

sardines sardeen

satisfactory: this is not satisfactory da mIyuhrdeesh

Saturday yum e-sabt

sauce salsa

saucepan Hala

saucer taba' fingāl

Saudi (*man, adjective*) sa*oodee; (*woman*) sa*oodaya

Saudi Arabia e-so*daya

sauna 'sauna'

sausage soogo'

sauté potatoes bataatis sōtay

save (*life*) uhnkuhz

savo(u)ry (*noun*) fateH li shaHaya

say: how do you say ... in Arabic? izzay ti'ool ... bil *arabee?; **what did you say?** olt ay?; **what did he say?** hoowa al ay?; **I said ...** ana olt ...; **he said ...** hoowa al ...; **I wouldn't say no** (*yes please*) lowsamaHt

scald: he's scalded himself hoowa Hara' nafsoo

scarf (*for neck*) talfeeHa; (*for head*) asharb

scarlet aHmar zēhee

scenery manzuhr

scent (*perfume*) reeHa

schedule gadwel

scheduled flight reHla *adaya

school madrassa; (*university*) koolaya;

I'm still at school ana lessa fil madrassa

science *Ilm

scissors: a pair of scissors ma'ass

scooter (*motor scooter*) 'scooter'

scorching: it's really scorching (*weather*) dee Harr fazee-a* awee

score: what's the score? e-nateega ay?

scorpion *a'ruhb

scotch (*whisky*) 'whisky'

Scotch tape (*tm*) shireet laz' sulōfān

Scotland eskotlanda

Scottish eskotlandee

scrambled eggs bayd ma'lee

scratch (*noun*) khadsh; **it's only a scratch** da khadsh baseet

scream (*verb*) sarakh

screw (*noun*) moosmarr alawawz

screwdriver mafak

scrubbing brush (*for hands*) forshit dawaafir; (*for floors*) forshit balaat

scruffy (*appearance, hotel*) mush nedeef; (*person*) mush nazeeh

scuba diving 'scuba diving'

sea baHr; **by the sea** ganb el baHr

sea air nismit el baHr

seafood samak

seafood restaurant mat*am asmak

seafront wag-hit el baHr; **on the seafront** *ala wag-hit el baHr

seagull noruhs

search (*verb*) fatish; **I searched everywhere** fatisht fee kuloo Hetta

search party fer'it tafteesh

seashell suhduhfa

seasick: I feel seasick Hassis bidookha; **I get seasick** baHass bidowaraan

seaside: by the seaside ganb el bilasH; **let's go to the seaside** yalla nerooH lil bilasH

season moosim; **in the high season** fil moosim; **in the low season** mush fil moosim

seasoning tawēbil

seat korsee; **is this anyone's seat?** Had a*Id hena?

seat belt Hezamil korsee; **do you have to wear a seat belt?** lezim testa*mil el неzam?

sea urchin onfid el baнr

seaweed *oshb baнree

secluded mon*azil

second (*adjective*) e-tanee; (*of time*) sanya; **just a second!** estanna shwıya!; **can I have a second helping?** mumkin tanee?

second class (*travel*) daraga tania

second-hand moosta*mil

secret (*noun*) sirr

secretary sekretēra (*f*)

sedative moosakin

see shēf; **I didn't see it** ana mashuftoohoosh; **have you seen my husband?** shuft goozee?; **I saw him this morning** ana shuftoo e-subнaya; **can I see the manager?** mumkin ashoof el modeer?; **see you tonight!** ashoofak bil layl!; **can I see?** mumkin aboss?; **oh, I see** (*I understand*) ıwa; **will you see to it?** (*arrange it*) mumkin terratibboo?

seldom nēdir

self-catering apartment sha'a mafroosha

self-service khedma zātaya

sell be-a*; **do you sell ...?** betbee-a* ...?; **will you sell it to me?** mumkin tebe-a*hālee?

sellotape (*tm*) shireet laz' sulōfān

send ba*at; **I want to send this to England** *a-ıyiz aba*at da lingilterra; **I'll have to send this food back** lezim araga* el akli da

senior: Mr Ahmed senior aнmed el kebeer

senior citizen *agooz

sensational (*holiday, experience etc*) momtaz

sense: I have no sense of direction ma*andeesh fikra *an el itigahat; **it doesn't make sense** da maloosh ma*ana

sensible (*person*) *a'il; (*idea*) kwıyis

sensitive (*person, skin*) нassēs

sentimental *aatifee

separate monfasil; **can we have separate bills?** mumkin tefsil el

fawateer?

separately: we're paying separately kuloo waaннid нıedfa* li nafsoo; **we're travel(l)ing separately** kuloo waaнid нısēfir li waнdō

September sibtimbuhr

septic ma*afin

serious (*person*) guhd; (*situation, problem, illness*) khoteer; **I'm serious** ana bakallim guhd; **you can't be serious!** inta bit-huhzuhr!; **is it serious, doctor?** da khoteer, ya doktor?

seriously: seriously ill *ıyān awee

servant khadam

service: the service was excellent el khedma kanit momtāza; **could we have some service, please!** mumkin tēkhud e-tuhluhb lowsamaнt?; **church service** suhla fil kineesa; **the car needs a service** el *arabaya meнtaga kashf *am

service charge (*in restaurant*) rasm el khedma

service station maнattit benzeen

serviette foota

set: it's time we were setting off el mafrood eнna kunna mashyeen delwa'tee

set menu kımit to*aam moнadadda

settle up: can we settle up now? mumkin nedfa* delwa'tee?

several keteer

sew khıyat; **could you sew this back on?** mumkin tekhıyat da?

sex (*sexual intercourse*) gins

sexy moghree

shade: in the shade fi dil

shadow khayēl

shake: let's shake hands yalla nesallim

shallow (*water*) mush ghaweet

shame: what a shame! yādil *ar!

shampoo (*noun*) shamboo; **can I have a shampoo and set?** ana *ıza shamboo wi tessreeн

share (*verb: room, table etc*) shērik; **let's share the cost** yalla nishērik el fatoora

shark samak ersh

sharp (*knife*) Hamee; (*taste*) Hareef; (*pain*) shedeed

shattered: I'm shattered (*very tired*) ana ta*ban awee

shave: I need a shave ana meHtag aHla' da'nee; **can you give me a shave?** mumkin teHle' da'nee?

shaver makanit Hila'a

shaving brush forshit Hila'a

shaving foam 'cream' Hila'a

shaving point bareeza li makanit el Hila'a

shaving soap sabōn Hila'a

shawl shēl

she haya; **is she here?** haya hena?; **is she a friend of yours?** haya saHibituhk?; **she's not English** haya mush ingileezaya; *see page 106*

sheep kharoof

sheet (*on bed*) millaya; (*of paper*) safHa; (*of glass etc*) lōH

sheikh shaykh

shelf ruhf

shell suhduhfa

shellfish suhduhfa

sherry 'sherry'

shingles marad el Hazba

ship safeena; **by ship** bi safeena

shirt amees

shit! ela*na!

shock (*surprise*) suhdma; **I got an electric shock from the ...** ana etkaharabt min ...

shock-absorber musa*adeen

shocking (*behaviour, prices, custom etc*) fazee-a*

shoe fardit gazma; **my shoes** gazmetee; **a pair of shoes** gazma

shoelaces roobaat gazma

shoe polish warneesh

shop maHal; (*small, local*) dokkān (*f*)

shopping: I'm going shopping rIaH ashteree Haggēt

shop window batreenit el maHal

shore (*of sea, lake*) shuht

short (*person, time, journey*) ōsIyar; **it's only a short distance** mush bay*eeda

short-change: you've short-changed me inta iditnee el feloos na'sa

short circuit dIra ōsIyara

shortcut taree' mokhtassir

shorter/shortest a'suhr

shorts short; (*underwear*) koolot

should: what should I do? *amil ay?; **he shouldn't be long** hoowa zamānoo gay; **you should have told me** el malfrood ennak oltillee

shoulder kitf

shoulder blade *admit kitāf

shout (*verb*) za*'

show: could you show me? mumkin toowareenee?; **does it show?** da bayn?; **we'd like to go to a show** *Izeen nerooH nitfaruhg *ala este*raad

shower (*in bathroom*) dōsh; **with shower** bee dōsh

showercap bonnay

show-off: don't be a show-off matitla*ash feeha awee

shrimps gambaree

shrine duhreeH

shrink: it's shrunk da kash

shut (*verb*) afal; **when do you shut?** biti'fil emta?; **when do they shut?** biyi'filoo emta?; **it was shut** kan afil; **I've shut myself out** el bab eta'fil wanna barra; **shut up!** ekhrus!; (*more polite*) oskut!

shutter (*on camera*) monazim fatHet el *adessa; (*on window*) sheesh

shy khagool

sick (*ill*) *Iyān; **I think I'm going to be sick** (*vomit*) ana Hassis ennee Hatrush

side gamb; (*in game*) faree'; **at the side of the road** *ala gamb e-taree'; **the other side of town** fee akhr el medeena

side lights e-noor el waatee

side salad salaata

side street shari'a gānebee

sidewalk raseef

sidewalk café ahwa

siesta raHa

sight: the sights of ... monaazeer el ...

sightseeing: sightseeing tour gowla see-aHaya; **we're going sightseeing** rIHeen fee gowla see-aHaya

sign (*roadsign etc*) ishaara; (*written character*) ramz; **where do I sign?** uhmdee fayn?

signal: he didn't give a signal (*driver, cyclist*) hoowa madēsh ishaara

signature emda

signpost yafta

silence hidoo'

silencer *albit e-shakmān

silk Hareer

silly (*person, thing to do etc*) sakheef; **that's silly!** da sakheef!

silver (*noun*) faada; (*adjective*) fidee

silver foil wara' fidee

similar zay

simple (*easy*) sahl

Sinai Peninsula seena

since: since yesterday min embarraH; **since we got here** min sa*It mageena hena

sincere mokhlis

sing ghenē

singer moghenee

single: a single room ōda lee waaHid; **a single to ...** tazkara lee ...; **I'm single** ana *azib

sink (*in kitchen*) Hōd; **it sank** gher'it

sir effendee; **excuse me, sir** lowsamaHt yaffendee

sirloin 'steak'

sister okht; **my sister** okhtee

sister-in-law: my sister-in-law (*wife's sister*) okht miraatee; (*husband's sister*) okht goozee

sit: may I sit here? mumkin a*ood hena?; **is anyone sitting here?** fee Had hena?

situation mowkif

size Hagm; (*of clothes*) ma'ass; **do you have any other sizes?** *andak ma'assat tania?

sketch (*noun*) 'sketch'

ski (*noun: for waterskiing*) 'ski'

skid: I skidded ana etzaHla't

skin gild

skin-diving 'skin diving'; **I'm going skin-diving** ana rIaH 'skin diving'

skinny naHeef awee

skirt goonilla

skull gomgomma

sky samma

sleep nam; **I can't sleep** mush a'dar anam; **did you sleep well?** nimt kwIyis?; **I need a good sleep** ana meHtag noom keteer

sleeper (*rail: whole train*) atr e-noom

sleeping bag kees linoom

sleeping car (*rail*) *arabayit noom

sleeping pill Habba minawimma

sleepy (*person*) na*asēn; (*weather, day*) minowim; (*town*) hadia; **I'm feeling sleepy** ana na*asēn

sleeve kum

slice (*noun*) Hetta

slide (*photography*) 'slide'

slim (*adjective*) naHeef; **I'm slimming** ana ba*mil resHeem

slip (*under dress*) amees taHtanee; **I slipped** (*on pavement etc*) etzaHla't

slipped disc inzilluhk ghadroofee

slippers ship ship

slippery mizaHla'; **it's slippery** mizHla'a

slow batee'; **slow down!** (*driving*) hadee e-sor*a!; (*speaking*) ēhda!

slowly baraHa; **could you say it slowly?** mumkin ti'oloo baraHa?; **very slowly** baraHa awee

small sooghIar

smaller/smallest uhsghar

small change fakka

smallpox el gudaree

smart (*clothes*) uhneek

smashing (*holiday, time, food etc*) gameel

smell: there's a funny smell fee reeHa ghereeba; **what a lovely smell!** reeHa Helwa awee!; **it smells** (*smells bad*) reeHa weHsha

smile (*verb*) ebtasuhm

smoke (*noun*) dokhan; **do you smoke?** bidakhan?; **do you mind if I smoke?** mumkin adakhan?; **I don't smoke** mabadakhansh

smooth (*surface*) na*Im

snack: I'd just like a snack ana *a-ɪyiz tuhsbeera

snackbar 'cafeteria'

snake te*aban

sneakers gazma kawetsh

snob mitkuhbuhr

snorkel 'snorkel'

snow (*noun*) talg

so: it's so hot ʜarr awee; **it was so beautiful!** kan gameel awee!; **not so fast** mush bisora*a; **thank you so much** shukran gazeelan; **it wasn't — it was so!** la' makensh — ɪwa kan; **so am I** ana kamēn; **so do I** ana kamēn; **how was it? — so-so** ay el akhbar? — nus-oo-nus

soaked: I'm soaked ana mablool

soaking solution (*for contact lenses*) maʜloof lituhndeef

soap sabōn

soap-powder mas-ʜoo' gheseel

sober (*not drunk*) razeen; (*serious*) gad

soccer kora kuhduhm

sock fardit sharab; **socks** sharab

socket (*electrical*) bareeza

soda (*water*) 'soda'

sofa kanaba

soft (*material etc*) na*ɪm

soft drink mashroob gheer kaʜolee

soldier *askaree

sole (*of shoe*) na*l; (*of foot*) batn e-rigl; **could you put new soles on these?** mumkin terakib na*l gedeed lee dōl?

solid gāmid

Somalia e-somaal

Somalian somaalee

some: may I have some water? mumkin shwɪyt mɪya?; **do you have some matches?** ma*ak kabreet?; (*in a shop*) *andak kabreet?; **that's some drink!** da mashroob tamam awee!; **some of them** ba*dōhum; **can I have some?** (*small amount of cheese etc*) mumkin akhud shwɪya?; **can I have some** (*oranges etc*) mumkin (bortoo'aan *etc*)?; *see page 102*

somebody, someone ʜad

something ʜaga; **something to drink** ʜaga ashrabha

sometime: sometime this afternoon ba*d e-dohr

sometimes aʜeeyēnan

somewhere: somewhere in the room fil ōda; **I put it down somewhere** ana ʜatēttoo fee maken

son ibn; **my son** ibnee

song oghnaya

son-in-law gooz bint; **my son-in-law** gooz bintee

soon ʜālan; **I'll be back soon** ʜarga* bisora*; **as soon as you can** bee-asra* mɪyumkin

sore: it's sore bitewga*

sore throat: I have a sore throat *andee waga* fi zor

sorry: (I'm) sorry asif; **sorry?** (*didn't understand*) na*m?

sort: what sort of ...? ay nōa* ...?; **a different sort of ...** nōa* tanee min ...; **will you sort it out?** mumkin teʜeloo?

soup shorba

sour (*taste*) haamid

source of the Nile mamba* e-neel

south ganoob; **to the south** lil ganoob

South Africa ganoob afrikia

South African (*adjective, person*) min ganoob afrikia

southeast el ganoob e-shar'ee; **to the southeast** lil ganoob e-shar'ee

southwest el ganoob el gharbee; **to the southwest** lil ganoob el gharbee

souvenir tizkaar

spa yanbooa*

space heater sakhēn kaharaba

spade (*tool*) ma*za'a

spades (*cards*) buhstōnee

Spain esbania

spanner muftaʜ ingileezee

spare part kitta*it gheeyar

spare tyre/tire *agala estebn

spark(ing) plug boosʜeehat

speak: do you speak English? bitikallim ingileezee?; **I don't speak ...** ana mabakallimsh ...; **can I speak to ...?** mumkin akallim ...?; **speaking** (*on telephone*) bikallim

special khosoosee; **nothing special** *adee

specialist mokhtuhs

special(i)ty: the special(i)ty of the house akl maнallee

spectacles nuhdaara

speed (noun) sora*a; **he was speeding** hoowa kan saye' bisora*a

speedboat luhnsh

speed limit e-sora*a el *ozma

speedometer *adad e-sora*a

spend saraf; **I've spent all my money** saraft kul feloosee

sphinx abul hōl

spice booharr

spicy: it's very spicy Hāmee awee

spider *ankaboot

splendid (very good) momtaz

splint (for broken limb) gabeera

splinter (in finger) shazee-a

splitting: I've got a splitting headache *andee suda* shedeed

spoke (in wheel) silk

sponge safinga

spoon ma*le'a

sport reeyaada

sport(s) jacket sнakit

spot (on face etc) dimil; **will they do it on the spot?** Hıya*miloo fee wa'taha?

sprain: I've sprained my ... ana lawayt ...

spray (for hair) bakhēkhēh

spring (season) e-rabee-a*; (of car, seat) sosat

square (in town) midan; **ten square metres** *ashara mitr mooruhba*

squash (sport) 'squash'

stain (noun: on clothes) bo'a*a

stairs sallēlim (f)

stale (bread, taste) mush taaza

stall: the engine keeps stalling el mator bee'ata*

stalls (in theatre) saala

stamp (noun) taabea*; **a stamp for England, please** taabea* lingilterra, lowsamaнt

stand: I can't stand ... (can't tolerate) mush a'dar atнamil ...

standard (adjective) mustowa

standby 'waiting list'

star (in sky) nigma; (person) nigm

start (noun) el beedaya; **when does the film start?** el film beeyebda' emta?; **the car won't start** el *arabaya mabidorsh

starter (of car) el marsh; (food) fateн lil shahaya

starving: I'm starving ana mayit min el goo-a*

state (in country) willaya; **the States** (USA) amreeka

station (train) maнattit e-sikka el нadeed; (bus) mow'af el ōtōbeesēt

statue timsēl

stay: we enjoyed our stay eнna enbassuhtna awee; **where are you staying?** inta nezil fayn?; **I'm staying at ... a**na nezil fee ...; **I'd like to stay another week** *a-ıyiz a*od isboo*a tanee; **I'm staying in tonight a**na mush khērig elleelādee

steak 'steak'

steal sere'; **my bag has been stolen** shantitee etsere'it

steep (hill) нād

steering e-drikseeyōn; **the steering is slack** e-drikseeyōn bee fawit

steering wheel itar e-drikseeyōn

step (in front of house etc) buнsta

stereo 'stereo'

sterling estirleenee

steward (on plane) modeef

stewardess modeefa

sticking plaster blastar

sticky: it's sticky da milaza'

sticky tape shireet laza'

still: I'm still waiting ana lessa mistanee; **will you still be open?** нatkoon lessa fateн?; **it's still not right** da lessa mush tamem; **that's still better** da aнsen; **keep still!** ō'af sēbit

sting: a bee sting arsit naнla; **I've been stung a**na et'aruhst

stink (noun) reeнa weнsha; **it stinks** reeнtoo waнesh awee

stockings sharab feellay

stolen masroo'; **my wallet's been**

stolen maнfuhztee etsara'it

stomach me*ada; **do you have something for an upset stomach?** *andak нaga lee waga* el me*ada?

stomach-ache maghas

stone (*rock*) нaguhr; *see page 118*

stop (*bus stop*) maнattit ōtōbees; **which is the stop for ...?** fayn el maнatta lee ...?; **please, stop here** (*to taxi driver etc*) нena lowsamaнt; **do you stop near ...?** bitō'af orɪyib min ...?; **stop doing that!** buhtuhl da!

stopover 'transit'

store (*shop*) maнal; (*small, local*) dokkān (*f*)

stor(e)y (*of building*) dor

storm *asifa

story (*tale*) kissa

stove forn

straight (*road etc*) mustakeem; **it's straight ahead** *alatool; **straight away** fowran; **a straight whisky** 'whisky' li waнdo

straighten: can you straighten things out? (*sort things out*) mumkin tefuhdee ishkal?

strange (*odd*) ghereeb; (*unknown*) ghereeb

stranger ghereeb; **I'm a stranger here** ana mush min нena

strap (*on watch*) ōstayk; (*on dress, on suitcase*) нēzam

strawberry farowla

streak (*in hair*) mashēt; **could you put streaks in?** mumkin mashēt fi sha*r?

stream magra

street shari*a; **on the street** fi shari*a

street café ahwa

streetcar tromɪ

streetmap khareetit toro'

strep throat waga* zor

strike (*noun*) idraab; **are they on strike?** fee idraab?; **they're on strike** modribeen *an e-shoghl

string doobaara; **have you got some string?** (*in a shop*) *andak doobaar?; (*to a person*) ma*ak doobaar?

striped ma'allim

stroke: he's just had a stroke gatlō

zabнa sadraya

stroll: let's go for a stroll yalla nuhkhrug nitmasha

stroller (*for babies*) *arabit tefl

strong (*person, voice*) shedeed; (*taste, curry*) нāmee; (*drink*) morakaz

stroppy (*official, waiter*) *ɪnadee

stuck maznoo'; **the key's stuck** el muftaн etzana'

student (*male*) taalib; (*female*) taalibba

stuffed vine leaves wara' *ɪnab

stupid ghebee; **that's stupid** da ghebē'

sty(e) (*in eye*) ramad нobaybee

subtitles targamma

suburb dawaнee

subway (*underground*) nafa'

successful: were you successful? inta etwafa't?

Sudan e-soodan

Sudanese (*man, adjective*) soodānee; (*woman*) soodanaya

suddenly fag'a

sue: I intend to sue нarfa* da*wa

suede shamwa

Suez Canal konat e-seewis

sugar sukar; **without sugar** sēda

sugar cane asab

suggest: what do you suggest? ra'yak ay?

suit (*noun*) badla; **it doesn't suit me** mabit nasibneesh; **it suits you** нelwa *aleek; **that suits me fine** da yirdeenee awee

suitable (*time, place*) monāsib

suitcase shantit safar

sulk: he's sulking hoowa mibowiz

sultan sultaan

sultana (*wife of sultan*) sultaana

sultry (*weather, climate*) rōtooba *alee-a

summer si-if; **in the summer** fi si-if

sun shams (*f*); **in the sun** fi shams; **out of the sun** fi dil; **I've had too much sun** ana нassis bee darbit shams

sunbathe etshamis

sunblock (*cream*) 'cream' duhd e-shams

sunburn lafнet shams

sunburnt maнroo' min e-shams
Sunday yum el Had
sunglasses naddara shamsaya
sun lounger (*chair*) korsee lil bilasн
sunny: if it's sunny low mishamissa;
 a sunny day yum mishamis
sunrise shiroo' e-shams
sun roof (*in car*) sa'f motaнarig
sunset ghroob e-shams
sunshade shamsaya
sunshine shoo*a* e-shams
sunstroke darbit shams
suntan suhmar min e-shams
suntan lotion lōshan li shams
suntanned ismar min e-shams; **I'm
 suntanned** ana esmareet min e-
 shams
suntan oil zayt li shams
sun worshipper *abeed e-shams
super (*time, holiday*) lazeez; (*person*)
 momtaz; **super!** momtaz!
superb (*buildings, sunsets, view*) rowa*a
supermarket 'supermarket'
supper *asha
supplement (*extra charge*) rasm
 idaafee
suppose: I suppose so a*tuhkid
 kedda
suppository om*a
sure: I'm sure ana muta'akid; **are
 you sure?** inta muta'akid?; **he's sure**
 hoowa muta'akid; **sure!** ō kay!
surf 'surf'
surfboard 'surfboard', loн enzilaak
surfing: I want to go surfing ana *a-
 ıyiz 'surfing'
surname ism el ıayla
surprise (*noun*) mufag'a
surprising: that's not surprising da
 kan muta wokea*
suspension (*of car*) sōset

swallow (*verb*) bala*
swearword shiteema
sweat (*verb*) *ari'; (*noun*) *ara';
 covered in sweat *ar'ēn
sweater soo-wētuhr
sweatshirt fanilla
Sweden e-sweed
sweet (*taste*) нelw; (*noun: dessert*) нelw
sweets нalawee-at
swelling waram
sweltering: it's sweltering dee нarr
 awee
swerve: I had to swerve (*when driving*) etuhrit анowid bisora*a
swim (*verb*) *am; **I'm going for a
 swim** ana rıнa a*-oom; **do you want
 to go for a swim?** inta *a-ıyiz terooн
 te*-oom?; **I can't swim** ma*arafsh
 a*-oom
swimming sibāнa; **I like swimming**
 ana baнebb e-sibāнa
swimming costume mayō нareemee
swimming pool нammem sibāнa
swimming trunks mayō rigālee
Swiss swisree
switch (*noun*) muftaн; **could you
 switch it on?** (*radio, TV, lights*)
 mumkin tewal*ow?; (*engines,
 machines*) mumkin tesheghelha?;
 could you switch it off? (*radio, TV,
 lights*) mumkin tetfeeh?; (*engines,
 machines*) mumkin tibatuhlha?
Switzerland swissra
swollen wērim
swollen glands ghōdad werma
sympathy *aatf
synagogue ma*abad yahoodee
synthetic estina*ı
Syria suree-a
Syrian (*man, adjective*) sooree; (*woman*)
 sooraya

table 60 telephone box/booth

T

table tarabayza; a table for two tarabayza litneen; at our usual table *and e-tarabayza el mo*atēda
tablecloth mafrash tarabayza
table tennis bing bong
table wine nebeet
tactful (person) labik
tailback (of traffic) taboor *arabeeyaat
tailor tarzee
take khad; will you take this to room 12? mumkin tekhud da lee ōda itnaashar?; will you take me to the airport? mumkin tekhudnee lil mataar?; do you take credit cards? bitekhud 'credit card'?; OK, I'll take it 'OK' Hakhdō; how long does it take? bitekhud ad ay?; it'll take 2 hours Hawalee sa*atayn; is this seat taken? fee Had a*ad hena?; I can't take too much sun ma'adarsh a*ood keteer fi shams; will you take this back, it's broken mumkin teraga* da, da maksoor?; could you take it in at the side? (dress, jacket) mumkin tikassim el ginab shwIya?; when does the plane take off? e-tIyara ma*adha emta?; can you take a little off the top? (to hairdresser) mumkin te'oss shwIya sooghIyara min fo'?
talcum powder budrit talk
talk (verb) etkallim
tall (person) taweel; (building) *alee
taller/tallest atwuhl
tampax 'tampax' (tm)
tampons 'tampax' (tm)
tan (noun) samar min e-shams; I want to get a good tan ana *a-Iyiz asmar min e-shams
tank (of car) 'tank'
tap Hanafaya

tape (for cassette) 'cassette'; (sticky) shireet laza'
tape measure mazoora
tape recorder rekordar
taste (noun) ta*m; can I taste it? mumkin adoo'oo?; it has a peculiar taste ta*moo ghereeb; it tastes very nice ta*moo Helw awee; it tastes revolting ta*moo waHesh awee
taxi taks; taxi! taks, taks!; will you get me a taxi? mumkin tegiblee taks?
taxi-driver sawē' taks
taxi rank, taxi stand mow'af takseeyet
tea (drink) shay; tea for two please shay litneen lowsamaHt; could I have a cup of tea? mumkin kubayit shay?
teabag kees shay
teach: could you teach me? mumkin te*alimnee?; could you teach me Arabic? mumkin te*alimnee *arabee?
teacher (male) mōdaris; (female) mōdarissa
team faree'
teapot baraad shay
tea towel foota
teenager (male) moraahik; (female) moraahikka
teetotal: he's teetotal hoowa mabyeshrabsh khaalis
telegram teleghraaf; I want to send a telegram ana *a-Iyiz aba*t teleghraaf
telephone telefōn; can I make a telephone call? mumkin asta*mil e-telefōn?; could you talk to him for me on the telephone? mumkin tekallimoo fi telefōn *alashēnee?
telephone box/booth kabeenit telefōn

telephone directory daleel telefōnet

telephone number rakuhm e-telefōn; **what's your telephone number?** nimrit telefōnak kam?

telephoto lens *adaset tuhsweer

television teleevizyōn; **I'd like to watch television** ana *a-ıyiz atfaruhg *ala e-teleevizyōn; **is the match on television?** el muhtsh fi teleevizyōn?

tell: could you tell him ...? mumkin ti'olloo ...?

temperature (*weather*) dargit el Harara; (*fever*) Homma; **he has a temperature** *andoo Homma

temple (*religious*) ma*abad; **Hatshepsut's temple** dē-ir el baHaree

temporary mo'uhkuht

tenant (*of apartment*) musta'gir

tennis 'tennis'

tennis ball korit 'tennis'

tennis court mala*b 'tennis'; **can we use the tennis court?** mumkin nista*mil mala*b e-'tennis'?

tennis racket muhdruhb 'tennis'

tent khayma

term (*at university, school*) fasl

terminus (*rail*) mow'af

terrace varanduh; **on the terrace** fil varanduh

terrible (*weather, food, accent*) fazee-a*

terrific (*weather, food, teacher*) momtaz

testicle khisya

than min; **smaller than** uhsghar min; **bigger than** uhkbar min

thanks, thank you shukran; **thank you very much** shukran gazeelan; **thank you for everything** shukran *ala kulla Haga; **no thanks** la' mutsheka

that: that woman e-sittee dee; **that man** e-raagil da; **that one** da/dee; **I hope that ...** atmana en ...; **that's perfect** da tamem; **that's strange** da ghereeb; **is that ...?** da ...?; **that's it** (*right*) saH!; **is it that expensive?** da ghēlee?; *see pages 106, 107*

the el; *see page 102*

theater, theatre masraH

their: their address *ınwanhum;

their house bayt-hum; *see page 105*

theirs bita*hum; *see page 108*

them humma; **for them** leehum; **with them** ma*ahum; **I gave it to them** ana eddit-hulhum; **who? — them** meen? — humma; *see page 106*

then ba*dayn

there hinak; **over there** hinak; **up there** fo'; **is there ...?** fee ...?; **are there ...?** fee ...?; **there is ...** fee ...; **there are ...** fee ...; **there you are** (*giving something*) itfuhduhl

thermal spring *ın sukhna

thermometer tuhrmomituhr

thermos flask tuhrmos

thermostat (*in car*) thuhrmōstat

these dōl; **can I have these?** mumkin dōl?; *see pages 106, 107*

they humma; **are they ready?** humma gahzeen?; **are they coming?** humma gayeen?; *see page 106*

thick tekheen; (*stupid*) ghebee

thief Haraamee

thigh fakhd

thin roofıya*

thing Haga; **have you seen my things?** shuft Hagtee?; **first thing in the morning** (*very early*) e-subH badree

think fakuhr; **what do you think?** ay ra'yak?; **I think so** *ala mazon; **I don't think so** maftikersh; **I'll think about it** Hafuhkuhr fee

third-class darga talta

third party insurance ta'meen *ala el gheer

thirsty: I'm thirsty ana *atshaan

this: this hotel el fondō' da; **this town** el medeena dee; **this one** (*masculine noun*) da; (*feminine noun*) dee; **this is my wife** dee miraatee; **this is my favo(u)rite café** dee ahwitee el mifuhdulla; **is this yours?** da bita*ak?; *see pages 106, 107*

those dōl; **not these, those** mush dōl, dōl; *see pages 106, 107*

thread (*noun*) alawawz

throat zor

throat lozenges bastilya

throttle (*on motorbike*) khēni

through: does it go through Tanta? beey*adee *ala tuhntuh?; **Monday through Friday** min yum el itneen lee yum el gom*a; **straight through the city centre** *alatool fee nus el balad

through train atr tawaalee

throw (*verb*) rama; **don't throw it away** matermihash; **I'm going to throw up** ana Hatrush

thumb e-sooba* el kebeer

thumbtack daboos

thunder (*noun*) ra*ad

thunderstorm bar' wi ra*ad

Thursday yum el khamees

ticket (*for bus, train, plane, cinema, cloakroom*) tazkara

ticket office (*bus, rail*) maktab e-tazēkir

tie (*noun: around neck*) garafatta

tight (*clothes etc*) dıye'; **the waist is too tight** el wist dıye' awee

tights sharab fee-lay

time wa't; **what's the time?** e-sa*a kam?; **at what time do you close?** bite'fil e-sa*a kam?; **there's not much time** mafeesh wa't; **for the time being** delwa'tee; **from time to time** min wa't lee tanee; **right on time** *alel ma*ad bizobt; **this time** el maraadee; **last time** el mara ellee fatit; **next time** el mara e-gaya; **four times** arba*a maraat; **have a good time!** atmanna lak wa't sa*yeed; *see page 116*

timetable gadwil el mo*a-ıd

tin (*can*) *alba

tinfoil wara' fidee

tin-opener fateHit *ılab

tint (*verb: hair*) lowin

tiny sooghıyar awee

tip (*to waiter etc*) ba'sheesh

tire (*for car*) kawetsh *arabaya

tired ta*aben; **I'm tired** ana ta*aben

tiring mot*ıb

tissues kliniks

to: to Egypt/to England li masr/lingilterra; **to London** lee 'london';

to the airport lil mataar; **here's to you!** (*toast*) fee saHetuhk!; *see page 116*

toast (*bread*) 'toast'; (*drinking*) nakhb

tobacco dokhēn

tobacconist, tobacco store maHal sagayar

today e-naharda; **today week** isboo-a* min e-naharda

toe sooba* rigl

toffee 'toffee'

together ma*aba*d; **we're together** eHna ma*aba*d; **can we pay together?** mumkin nitfa* fatoora waHda?

toilet tawalet; **where's the toilet?** fayn e-tawalet?; **I have to go to the toilet** ana lēzim arooH li tawalet; **she's in the toilet** haya fi tawalet

toilet paper wara' tawalet

toilet water kolonya

tomato oota

tomato juice *aseer oota

tomato ketchup 'ketchup'

tomb ma'barra

tomorrow bukra; **tomorrow morning** bukra e-subH; **tomorrow afternoon** bukra e-dohr; **tomorrow evening** bukra bil layl; **the day after tomorrow** ba*d bukra; **see you tomorrow** ashoofak bukra

ton tin; *see page 118*

tongue lissan

tonic (*water*) mıya ma*danaya

tonight elleelādee, el layla dee; **not tonight** mush elleelādee

tonsillitis eltihab el lēwaz

tonsils el lēwaz

too (*excessively*) awee; (*also*) kamēn; **too hot** Harr awee; **too much** keteer awee; **me too** ana kamēn; **I'm not feeling too good** ana mush kwıyis

tooth sinna

toothache waga* seenan

toothbrush forshit seenan

toothpaste ma*goon asnan

top: on top of ... fo' el ...; **on top of the car** fo' el *arabaya; **on the top floor** fil dor el akheer; **at the top**

fo'; **at the top of the tower** fo' el
borg; **top quality** sanf momtaz;
bikini top beekeenee
torch bataraya
total (*noun*) magmoo-a*
touch (*verb*) lamas; **let's keep in
touch** dawim el gawabēt
tough (*meat etc*) gamid; **tough luck!**
ma*alesh!
tour (*noun*) gowla; **is there a tour of
...?** fee gowla lee ...?
tour guide morshid seeyaнee
tourist sayaн
tourist information office maktab e-
seeyaнa
tourist police bolees e-seeyaнa
touristy seeyeнee; **somewhere not so
touristy** makan mush seeyeнee
tour operator maktab seeyaнa
tow: can you give me a tow? mumkin
teshadnee?
**toward(s): Tanta is toward(s) Alex-
andria** tuhntuh teega iskindraya;
**I'm travel(l)ing toward(s) Alex-
andria** ana misāfir iskindraya
towel foota
town medeena; **in town** fee nus el
balad; **which bus goes into town?**
ōtōbees kam beerooн li nus el
balad?; **we're staying just out of
town** eнna sekneen fee dawaнee el
medeena
town hall mabna el moнafzuh
tow rope нabl
toy le*aba
trachoma ramuhd нobaybee
track suit tiring
traditional aslee; **a traditional
Egyptian meal** akla masraya; **a
traditional restaurant** mata*m
shar'ee; **traditional costume** zay
masree aslee
traffic muhroor (*f*)
traffic cop *askaree muhroor
traffic jam zaнmit muhroor
traffic light(s) isharaat el muhroor
trailer (*for carrying tent etc*) ma'toora
train atr; **when's the next train to ...?**
emta ma*ad el atr lil ...; **by train** bil

atr
trainers (*shoes*) gazma kawetsh
train station maнattit atr
tram tromi
tramp (*person*) raнaal
tranquillizers mohadee
transfer desk maktab e-taнweelēt
transformer (*electrical*) tarans
transistor (*radio*) radee-ō tranzistor
transit lounge (*at airport*) saalit e-
transit
translate tergim; **could you translate
that?** mumkin tetargim da?
translation targamma
translator motargim
transmission (*of car*) na'l el нarikuh
travel safuhr; **we're travel(l)ing
around** eнna binit gowil
travel agent wikālit suhfuhr
travel(l)er musēfir
traveller's cheque, traveler's check
sheek seeyaнee
tray sanaya
treasure kinooz (*f*)
tree shuhgara
tremendous momtaz
trendy (*person, clothes, restaurant*)
sнims
tribe kaabeela
tribesman waaнid min el kaabeela
tricky (*difficult*) sa*ab
trim: just a trim please (*to hairdresser*)
uhs buhseet lowsamaнt
trip (*journey*) reнla; **I'd like to go on
a trip to ...** ana *a-ıyiz atla* reнla
lee ...; **have a good trip** reнla
sa*yeeda
tripod (*for camera*) нāmil bitalluht
rigool
tropical (*heat, climate*) istoo-wē'ee
trouble (*noun*) mashēkil; **I'm having
trouble with ...** ana *andee mashēkil
ma*a ...; **sorry to trouble you** asif lil
iz*ag
trousers bantalōn
trouser suit badla нareemee
truck looree
truck driver sawē' na'l
true нa'ee'ee; **that's not true** da mush

saн
trunk (*of car*) shanta; (*for belongings*) sandoo' нidoom
trunks (*swimming*) mayō rigālee
truth нa'ee'a; **it's the truth** dil нa'ee'a
try нawil; **please try** нawil lowsamaнt; **will you try for me?** mumkin teнawil *alashēnee?; **I've never tried it** (*food etc*) ana *omree magarabtoo; **can I have a try?** (*food*) mumkin adoo'oo?; (*at doing something*) mumkin agarab?; **may I try it on?** (*clothes*) mumkin a'eesoo
T-shirt amees nussa kom
tube (*for tyre*) etaar dakhilee
Tuesday yum e-talaat
tuition: I'd like tuition ana meнtag te*aleem
tuna fish samak toona
tune (*noun*) laнn
Tunis toonis
Tunisia toonis
Tunisian (*man, adjective*) toonissee; (*woman*) toonisaya
tunnel nafa'
Turkey torkaya

turkey deek roomee
Turkish delight malban
turn: it's my turn now da dooree ana; **turn left** нowid shimēl; **where do we turn off?** naнowid fayn?; **can you turn the air-conditioning on?** mumkin teshaghel e-takeef?; **can you turn the air-conditioning off?** mumkin tetfee e-takeef?; **he didn't turn up** hoowa magesh
turning (*in road*) taнweeda
TV teleevizyōn
tweezers mol'aat
twice maritayn; **twice as much** e-da*f
twin beds sireerayn
twin room ōda litneen
twins tow'am
twist: I've twisted my ankle ana lowayt ka*abee
type (*noun*) nōa*; **a different type of ...** nōa* tanee min ...
typewriter alakatba
typhoid tıfood
typical (*dish etc*) aslee; **that's typical!** da aslee!
tyre kawetsh

U

ugly (*person, building*) waнesh awee
ulcer orнa
Ulster irlanda e-shamalaya
umbrella shamsaya
uncle (*father's brother*) *am; (*mother's brother*) khel
uncomfortable (*chair etc*) mush moreeн
unconscious moghma *alay
under (*spatially*) taнt; (*less than*) a'el min
underdone (*meat*) nıya
underground (*rail*) nafa'
underpants koolot
undershirt fanilla

understand: I don't understand mush fēhim; **I understand** fēhim; **do you understand?** inta fēhim?
underwear malābis dakhilaya
undo (*clothes*) khala*
uneatable: it's uneatable mayitakelsh
unemployed *aatil
unfair: that's unfair da mush *adl
unfortunately lee soo'el нuz
unfriendly mush нebbee
unhappy нazeen
unhealthy (*person, climate etc*) mush seнe
United Arab Emirates el emiraat
United States amreeka; **in the**

United States fee amreeka
university gama*a
unlimited mileage (*on hire car*) masēfuh gheer maнdooda
unlock fataн; **the door was unlocked** el bab kan maftooн
unpack fak
unpleasant (*person, taste*) mush kwɪyis
unpronounceable: it's unpronounceable mush a'dar a'ooloo
untie fak
until laнad; **until we meet again** (*said as parting words*) laнad mānit'ābil tanee; **not until Wednesday** mush abl yum el arba*
unusual shez
up fo'; **further up the road** ō'dam shwɪya; **up there** fo'; **he's not up yet** (*not out of bed*) hoowa lessa masнeesh; **what's up?** (*what's wrong?*) fee ay?
upmarket (*restaurant, hotel, goods etc*)

ghēlee
Upper Egypt wag iblee, (*colloquial word*) e-sɪyeed
upset stomach waga* batn
upside down ma'loob
upstairs fo'
urgent mista*gil; **it's very urgent** da mōhim gidan gidan
urinary tract infection eltihab el masēna el bowlaya
us: with us ma*ana; **for us** *alashēnna; *see page 106*
use (*verb*) esta*mil; **may I use ...?** mumkin asta*mil ...?; **may I use the phone?** mumkin e-telefōn?
used: I used to swim a lot ana kunt ba*owm keteer; **when I get used to the heat** lamma ēkhud *alel нarr
useful mōfeed
usual *adee; **as usual** zay el *ada
usually *adetan
U-turn dowaraan lil khalf

V

vacancy: do you have any vacancies? (*hotel*) fee ewad fadee-a?
vacation agēzza; **we're here on vacation** eнna hena fee agēzza
vaccination tuht *ɪyeem
vacuum cleaner maknassa bil kaharaba
vacuum flask tuнrmos
vagina raнm
valid (*ticket etc*) salнa; **how long is it valid for?** salнa li'ad ay?
valley wēdee
Valley of the Kings wēdee el milook
valuable (*adjective*) sameen; **can I leave my valuables here?** mumkin aseeb momtallakaatee hena?
value (*noun*) eema
van *arabaya na'l
vanilla vanilla; **a vanilla ice cream**

sнelaatee vanilla
varicose veins dawēllee
variety show нaflit minawa*at
vary: it varies bitikh-telif
vase vaaza
vaudeville нaflit minawa*at
VD marad tanasollee
veal laнma kandooz
vegetables khōdar
vegetarian nabātee; **I'm a vegetarian** ana nabātee
veil нegab
velvet ateefa
vending machine makanit baya*
ventilator tahwaya
very awee; **very hot** sukhn awee; **just a very little Arabic** *arabee mokassuhr awee; **I only speak a very little Arabic** batkallim *arabee

shwɪya; **just a very little for me**
shwɪya sooghɪyara *alashēnee; **I like
it very much** ana baнebboo keteer
awee

vest (*under shirt*) fanilla; (*waistcoat*)
sideree

via *antuhree'; **via Cairo** *antuhree'
el kaheera

video (*noun*) 'video'

view manzar; **what a superb view!** da
manzar gameel awee!

viewfinder (*of camera*) zaabit el
manzar

villa villa

village kareeya

vine *ɪnab

vinegar khel

visa 'visa'

visibility (*for driving*) rō'ya

visit (*verb*) zar; **I'd like to visit ...** ana
*a-ɪyiz azor ...; **come and visit us**
ebba te*ala zorna

vital: it's vital that ... da mōhim in ...

vitamins vitameen

vodka 'vodka'

voice sōt

voltage volt

vomit (*verb*) tarash; (*noun*) toraash

wafer (*with ice cream*) baskaweeta

waist wist

waistcoat sideree

wait estanna; **wait for me** estannēnee;
don't wait for me matistanneesh; **it
was worth waiting for** fe*alan kan
yistaнa' el intizar; **I'll wait until my
wife comes** ana нastanna miraatee;
I'll wait a little longer нastanna
shwɪya kamen; **can you do it while
I wait?** mumkin ta*miloo wana
hena?; **wait a minute** estanna shwɪya

waiter garsōn; **waiter!** lowsamaнt!

waiting room нogrit el intizar

waitress garsōna; **waitress!**
lowsamaнt!

wake: will you wake me up at 6.30?
mumkin tessaнeenee e-sa*a sitta wa
nus?

Wales 'wales'

walk: let's walk there yalla nimshee;
is it possible to walk there?
mumkin atmashēha?; **I'll walk back**
нarga* mashee; **is it a long walk?**
haya masēfa too-weela?; **it's only a
short walk** da mush ba*yeed; **I'm
going out for a walk** ana kherig

atmasha; **let's take a walk around
town** yalla nitmasha fil balad

walking stick *okez

walkman (*tm*) kassit sooghɪyar

wall нayta

wallet maнfuнza

**wander: I like just wandering
around** ana baнebb atfaruhg

want: I want a ... (*said by man*) ana
*a-ɪyiz ...; (*said by woman*) ana *a-ɪza
...; **I don't want any** mush *a-ɪyiz; **I
want to go home** ana *a-ɪyiz arooн;
I don't want to mush *a-ɪyiz; **he
wants to ...** hoowa *a-ɪyiz ...; **what
do you want?** *a-ɪyiz ay?

war нarb

ward (*in hospital*) *ambuhr

warm dēfee; **it's so warm today** e-
gow dēfee e-naharda; **I'm so warm**
ana dafeeyen awee

warning (*noun*) inzar

was: it was ... kan ...; **was it ...?** kan
...?; *see page 113*

wash (*verb*) ghesil; **I need a wash** ana
meнtag ashuhtuhf; **can you wash
the car?** mumkin teghsil el
*arabaya?; **can you wash these?**

mumkin teghsillee dōl?; **it'll wash off** Hatitla* fil gheseel
washcloth foota
washer (*for bolt etc*) gilbuh, warda
washhand basin Hōd
washing (*clothes*) gheseel; **where can I hang my washing?** anshur el gheseel fayn?; **can you do my washing for me?** mumkin teghsillee gheseelee?
washing machine ghasella
washing powder mas-Hoo' gheseel
washing-up: I'll do the washing-up ana Haghsil el mowi-een
washing-up liquid se'il lighesl e-soHoon
wasp duhboor
wasteful: that's wasteful da tabzeer
wastepaper basket salit el mohmeelet
watch (*wrist-*) sa*a; **will you watch my things for me?** mumkin tekhud bālak min Hagtee?; **I'll just watch** ana Hatfaruhg bass; **watch out!** Hasib!
watch strap ostayk sa*a
water mIya; **may I have some water?** mumkin shwIyit mIya?
water-bottle ezāzit mIya
watercolo(u)r alwān mIya
waterpipe (*to smoke*) sheesha
waterproof (*adjective*) duhd el mIya
waterski: I'd like to learn to waterski ana *a-Iyiz at*allim et-tazaHlo' *ala el mIya
waterskiing 'waterskiing'
water sports reeyaddeeyaat ma'aya
water wheel sa'ya
wave (*in sea*) mooga
way: which way is it? fee ay e-teega?; **it's this way** fil e-teega da; **it's that way** fil e-teega da; **could you tell me the way to ...?** mumkin te'ollee e-taree' lil ...?; **is it on the way to Alexandria?** da fi taree' iskindraya?; **you're blocking the way** inta sēdid e-taree'; **is it a long way to ...?** haya masēfa too-weela lil ...?; **would you show me the way to do it?** mumkin tewareenee izzay?; **do it this way** a*amiloo kedda; **no way!** abadan!

we eHna; *see page 106*
weak (*person*) dIf; (*drink*) khafeef
wealthy ghenee
weather gow; **what foul weather!** e-gow fazee-a*!; **what beautiful weather!** e-gow gameel!
weather forecast nashra gawaya
wedding Haflit gawaz
wedding anniversary *Iyeed e-zawag e-sanawee
wedding ring khētim e-gawaz; (*in Egypt also*) dibla
Wednesday yum el arba*
week isboo-a*; **a week (from) Sunday** yum el Had e-gay; **Monday week** yum litneen e-gay
weekend raHa isboo*Iya; **at/on the weekend** yum e-gom*a
weight wazn; **I want to lose weight** ana *a-Iyiz akhis shwIya
weight limit (*for baggage*) wazn magēnee; (*for bridge*) wazn masmooH
weird (*person, custom, thing to happen*) ghereeb
welcome: welcome to ... marHabban lil ...; **you're welcome** (*don't mention it*) *afwan
well: I don't feel well ana ta*ban shwIya; **I haven't been very well** ana kunt ta*ban shwIya; **she's not well** haya ta*banna shwIya; **how are you? — very well, thanks** (*said to man*) izzayak? — kwIyis; (*said to woman*) izzayik? — kwIyissa; **you speak English very well** inta bititkallim ingileezee kwIyis awee; **me as well** ana kamen; **well done!** mabrook!; **well well!** (*suprise*) Halla halla!
well-done (*meat*) mistoo-waya awee
Welsh ingileezee min 'wales'
were *see page 113*
west gharb; **to the west** lil gharb
Western afrangee
West Indian (*man, woman, adjective*) min guzur el hind el gharbaya
West Indies guzur el hind el gharbaya
wet mablool; **it's all wet** kuloo

mablool

wet suit (*for diving etc*) badlit ghats

what? ay?; **what's that?** edda?; **what is he saying?** hoowa bee'ool ay?; **I don't know what to do** ana mush *arif a*mil ay; **what a view!** manzar gameel!

wheel *agala

wheelchair korsee lil *agaza

when? emta?; **when does the bus come?** emta el ōtōbees gay?, el ōtōbees gay emta?; **when we get back** lamma nerga*; **when we got back** lamma riga*na

where? fayn?; **where is ...?** fayn ...?; **I don't know where he is** ana mush *arif hoowa fayn; **that's where I left it** (*pointing*) ana sibtoo hena

which aya; (*with numbered items*) kam; **which street?** aya shari*a?; **which hotel?** aya fondō'?; **which one?** aya waaнid?; **which bus number?** ōtōbees kam?; **which flight number?** reнla kam?; **which is yours?** fayn bita*k?; **I forget which it was** mush fēkhir aya waaнid; **the one which ...** el waaнid ellee ...

while (*conjunction*) wa; **while I'm here** wana hena

whisky 'whisky'

whisper (*verb*) washwish

white abeeyad

white wine nebeet abeeyad

who? meen?; **who was that?** meen da?; **the man who ...** e-raagil ellee ...

whole: the whole week el isboo-a* kuloo; **two whole days** yumayn kamleen; **the whole lot** kuloohum

whooping cough e-so*ıl e-deekee

whose: whose is this? da bita* meen?

why? lay?; **why not?** lay la'?, la' lay?; **that's why it's not working** da e-sabuhb ennoo mush shaghēl

wide *areed

wide-angle lens *adessa bizawee-a kebeera

widow armalla

widower armuhl

wife zōga; **my wife** miraatee; **your wife** miraatak

wig barooka

will: will you ask him? mumkin tis'alloo?; *see page 110*

win (*verb*) kisib; **who won?** meen kisib?

wind (*noun*) reeн (*f*)

window shebek; **near the window** gamb e-shebek; **in the window** (*of shop*) fil batreena

window seat korsee gamb e-shebek

windscreen, windshield barabreez amāmee

windscreen wipers, windshield wipers massaнat

windsurf: I'd like to windsurf ana *a-ıyiz 'windsurf'

windsurfing 'windsurfing'

windy howa shedeed; **it's so windy** e-reeн shedeeda awee

wine nebeet; **can we have some more wine?** mumkin nebeet tanee?

wine glass kas nebeet

wine list kımit e-nebeet

wing (*of plane, bird*) ginaн; (*of car*) ruhfruhf

wing mirror mirraya

winter shitta; **in the winter** fi shitta

winter holiday agēzza shitwaya

wire silk

wireless radyō

wiring silk el kaharaba

wish: best wishes aateeyuhb el amānee

with ma*; **with me** ma*aya; **with you** ma*ak; **I'm staying with ...** ana ē-ıd ma* ...; **with milk** bee laban

without min gheer

witness shēhid; **will you be a witness for me?** mumkin teshadlee?

witty zareef

wobble: it wobbles (*wheel*) mush mowzoona

woman sit

women sittāt

wonderful (*holiday, meal, weather, person*) modhish

won't: it won't start mabidorsh; *see*

page 110
wood (*material*) khashab
wool soof
word kelma; **you have my word** (*I promise*) awɪduhk
work (*verb*) ishtaghel; (*noun*) shoghl; **how does it work?** bitishtaghel izzay?; **it's not working** mush shaghel; **I work in an office** ana bashtaghel fee maktab; **do you have any work for me?** *andak shoghl laya?; **when do you finish work?** bitkhaalas shoghl emta?
world e-donya; **all over the world** fil *aluhm
worm (*parasitic*) dooda
worn-out (*person*) te*ɪb; (*shoes, clothes*) helkāna
worry: I'm worried about her ana el'ān *alayha; **don't worry** mate'la'sh
worry beads sebHa
worse: it's worse da aswuh'; **it's getting worse** da aswuh' min el owɪl
worst el aswuh'
worth: it's not worth 5 pounds da mɪ-istaHa'ish khamsa ginay; **it's worth more than that** da yistaHa' aktuhr min kedda; **is it worth a visit?** da yistaHa' e-zeeyara?
would: would you please ...? mumkin ...?; **would you give this to**

...? mumkin teddee da lee ...?; **what would you do?** Hata*mil ay?
wrap: could you wrap it up? mumkin telefoo?
wrapping laf
wrapping paper wara' lil laf
wrench (*tool*) muftaH ingileezee
wrist 'wrist'
write katab; **could you write it down?** mumkin tiktiboo?; **how do you write it?** tiktiboo izzay?; **I'll write to you** Haktiblak; **I wrote to you last month** ana katabtillak e-shahr elleefat
write-off: it's a write-off (*car etc*) matsaweesh Haga
writer kātib
writing kitāba; **Arabic writing** kitāba *arabaya
writing paper wara' lil kitāba
wrong: you're wrong inta ghaltaan; **the bill's wrong** el fatoora ghalat; **sorry, wrong number** asif, el nimra ghalat; **I'm on the wrong train** ana rikibt ghalat; **I went to the wrong room** ana roHt lee ōda tania; **that's the wrong key** mush da el muftaH; **there's something wrong with ...** fee *ɪyib fee ...; **what's wrong?** fee ay?; **what's wrong with it?** maloo?; **what's wrong with you?** malak?

X

X-ray esha*it 'X'

Y

yacht yakht
yacht club nēdee el yakht
yard: in the yard fil Hōsh; *see page 117*
year sana
yellow asfar
yellow fever Homa safra
yellow pages daleel telefōnet toogāree
Yemen: North Yemen el yemen e-shamalaya; South Yemen el yemen el ganoobaya
Yemeni (*man, adjective*) yamenee; (*woman*) yamanaya
yes ıwa
yesterday imbarraH; yesterday morning imbarraH e-subH; yesterday afternoon imbarraH e-dohr; the day before yesterday owel imbarraH
yet: has it arrived yet? wasuhl wala lessa?; not yet lessa

yobbo: he's a yobbo hoowa mushēghib
yog(h)urt zabādee
you (*to a man*) inta; (*to woman*) intee; (*plural*) intoo; this is for you da *alashēnak; with you ma*ak; *see page 106*
young sheb
young people shebeb
your: your house (*if owner male*) baytak; (*if owner female*) baytik; (*if referring to several people*) baytkoo; *see page 105*
yours (*if owner male*) da bita*ak; (*if owner female*) da bita*ik; (*if referring to several people*) da bita*akoo; *see page 108*
youth hostel bayt shebab; we're youth hostel(l)ing eHna beeno*d fee bayoot shebab
Yugoslavia yughoslavia

Z

zero sifr
zip, zipper sosta; could you put a new zip on? mumkin terakib sosta

gedeeda?
zoo gooninit el HIawanet
zoom lens *adessa 'zoom'

Arabic – English

The signs and notices that you encounter will be in formal, Classical Arabic, which is essentially a written language, rarely spoken and quite distinct from colloquial Egyptian Arabic. Do not be surprised, therefore, to find that the pronunciation reveals differences between items as they occur in the English-Arabic and the Arabic-English sections of this book. Notice also that Arabic script runs from right to left.

LIST OF SUBJECT AREAS

Abbreviations
Airport and plane
Banks
Bars
Buses
Bus station
Cinemas, movie theaters
Clothing labels
Countries and nationalities
Cultural and historical interest
Customs
Days of the week
Department store sections
Doctors
Do not ...
Drinks on menus
Eating and drinking places
Emergencies
Exclamations and swearwords
Food
Food labels
Forms
Garages
Geographical
Greetings
Hairdressers
Hospitals
Hotels
Medical

Medicine labels
Men's names
Months of the year
Movie theaters
Musicians, singers
Night spots
Notices in restaurants, bars, and on
　　menus
Notices in shops
Notices on doors and gates
Place names
Post office
Public buildings
Public holidays (Egyptian)
Railway station
Replies
Restaurants
Rest rooms
Road signs
Schedules
Shop names
Streets
Taxis
Telephones
Theatres, theaters
Timetables, schedules
Toilets, rest rooms
Tourism
Youth hostel

ABBREVIATIONS

سم centimetres, centimeters

جم gram(me)s

س hours

كجم kilogram(me)s

كم kilometres, kilometers

لتر litres, liters

م metres, meters

مجم milligram(me)s

سم³ millilitres, milliliters

مليم millimes

مم millimetres, millimeters

ق minutes

ؗ piastres (*100 piastres = 1 Egyptian pound*)

ح pounds (*Egyptian*)

B.C.C. Bank of Credit and Commerce

E.A.B. Egyptian American Bank

E.G.B. Egyptian Gulf Bank

I.C.I. International Language Centre/Center

I.L.I. International Language Institute

M.D.C. Masr (Egyptian) Development Company

N.E.C. Tele-masr Company, television and radio maufacture

J.V.C. Video Service Centre/Center

AIRPORT AND PLANE

وصول *[wisool]* arrivals

صالة الوصول *[saalit el wisool]* arrivals hall

بطاقة صعود *[bita'it so*ood]* boarding pass

النقد الأجنبي *[e-nuhkd el agnabee]* currency declaration office

صالة السفر *[saalit e-suhfuhr]* departure lounge

سوق حرة *[soo' Hora]* duty-free

للمصرين فقط *[lil masrayeen fakuht]* Egyptians only

رقم الرحلة *[rakuhm e-reHla]* flight number

للأجانب فقط *[lil agēnib fakuht]* foreigners only

استعلامات *[ista*lamat]* information

المفقودات *[el mafkoodet]* lost property, lost and found

رسائل *[rasē'il]* meeting point

ممنوع الدخول *[mamnoo-a* e-dikhool]* no entry

جوازات *[gawazēt]* passport control

خاص *[khaass]* private

العلاقات العامة *[el *Ilakaat el *ama]* public relations office

دورات المياه *[dawaraat el meeyē]*

toilets, rest rooms

مرحباً [marHabban] welcome

BANKS

بنك إسكندرية [bank iskindraya]
Bank of Alexandria

بنك القاهرة [bank el kaheera] Cairo
Bank

الخزينة [el khazeena] cashier

حسابات جارية [Hisabāt gareeya]
current account, checking account

قسم العملة الأجنبية [kism el
*omla el agnabaya] foreign
exchange

الكارت الذهبي [el kart e-zahibee]
golden card, an Egyptian bank
card

بنك مصر [bank masr] Misr Bank

البنك الأهلي المصري [el bank el
ahlee el masree] National Bank of
Egypt

قرش [kuhrsh; spoken: uhrsh]
piastre (100 piastres = 1 Egyptian
pound)

ﻙ piastres (abbreviation)

جنيه [ginay] pounds (Egyptian)

ﺡ pounds (abbreviation for
Egyptian pounds)

حسابات التوفير [Hisabāt
e-towfeer] savings

سحب [saHb] withdrawals

BARS see **DRINKS** and **NOTICES
IN RESTAURANTS, BARS**

BUSES

ممنوع التدخين [mamnoo-a*
e-tadkheen] no smoking

مخصص لكبار السن فقط
[mokhassuhs li kubaar e-sin]
reserved for the elderly

التدخين مخالف للقانون
[e-tadkheen mokhellif lil kaanoon]
smoking is against the law

BUS STATION

رصيف . . . [raseef ...] bay
no. ..., lane no. ...

محطة أتوبيس [maHattit ōtōbees] bus
stop

هيئة النقل العام [hI'it e-na'l
el *am] General Transport
Company

CINEMAS, MOVIE THEATERS

حجز تذاكر [Hagz tazēkir] advance
bookings

بلكون [balakōn] balcony

شباك التذاكر [shebek e-tazēkir]
box office

الرجا مراجعة التذاكر والنقود قبل
مغادرة الشباك [e-raga morag*It
e-tazēkir wa e-nikood abl
moghadrit e-shebek] check your

tickets and change before
leaving the box office

سينما ['cinema'] cinema, movie
theater

ممنوع الخروج الا بعد انتهاء
الفيلم [mamnoo-a* el khuroog illa
ba*d intiha' el film] don't leave
before the performance ends

خروج [khuroog] exit

فوتيه لوج [loSH] lounge

العرض القادم [el *ard el kaadim]
next show

ممنوع دخول المأكولات داخل
السينما [mamnoo-a* dikhool el
ma'koolet dekhil e-'cinema'] you
are not allowed to bring your own
food into the cinema/movie
theater

ممنوع التدخين داخل صالة العرض
[mamnoo-a* e-tadkheen
dekhil saalit el *ard] no smoking in
the auditorium

مواعيد الحفلات [mowa*Id el
Hafalet] performance times

حالياً [Halayan] showing now

صالة [saala] stalls

دورات المياه [dawaraat el meeyē]
toilets, rest rooms

CLOTHING LABELS

٤ age 4 years

صناعة مصرية [sina*a masraya]
Egyptian made

صنع في مصر [suna* fee masr]
made in Egypt

٤٤ size 44 (*British size 12*)

**COUNTRIES AND
NATIONALITIES**

الجزائر [el gazē-ir] Algeria

جزائرى [gaze-eeree] Algerian

أمريكا [amreeka] America

أمريكي [amreekee] American

البحرين [el baHrayn] Bahrain

مصر [masr] Egypt

مصري [masree] Egyptian

إنجلترا [ingilterra] England

إنجليزي [ingileezee] English

العراق [el *Irak; spoken: el *Ira']
Iraq

عراقي [*Irakee; spoken: *Ira'ee]
Iraqi

إسرائيل [isra-eel] Israel

إسرائيلي [isra-eelee] Israeli

الأردن [el ordun] Jordan

أردني [ordonnee] Jordanian

الكويت [koowayt] Kuwait

كويتي [koowaytee] Kuwaiti

لبناني [libnānee] Lebanese

لبنان [libnān] Lebanon

ليبيا [libya] Libya

ليبي [leebee] Libyan

مغربي [maghribee] Moroccan

المغرب [el maghrib] Morocco

عمان [*aman] Oman

فلسطين [falastseen] Palestine

فلسطيني [falasteenee] Palestinian

قطر [kuhtuhr; spoken: uhtuhr] Qatar

سعودي [sa*oodee] Saudi

السعودية [e-so*daya] Saudi Arabia

السودان [e-soodan] Sudan

سوداني [soodanee] Sudanese

سوريا [suree-a] Syria

سوري [sooree] Syrian

تونس [toonis] Tunisia

تونس [toonissee] Tunisian

تركيا [torkaya] Turkey

اليمن الشمالية [el yamen e-shamalaya] North Yemen

اليمن الجنوبية [el yamen e-ganoobaya] South Yemen

يمني [yamenee] Yemeni

CULTURAL AND HISTORICAL INTEREST

Islamic/religious

الله [allah] Allah

رب اجعل هذا بلداً آمناً [rab eg*al haza baladan aminan] Allah make this a safe country

الله أكبر [allah akbar; spoken: allah wa akbar] Allah is almighty

قبلة [ibla] direction of Mecca

بسم الله الرحمن الرحيم [bismillah e-raHman e-raHeem] in the name of God most merciful

جمعية الإخوان المسلمين [gam*Iyit el ekhwan el muslimeen] The Islamic Brotherhood

القرآن [el kur'aan] Koran

محمد [moHamed] Mohamed

الصبر جميل [e-sabr gameel] patience is beautiful

رمضان [ramadaan] Ramadan

لا إله إلا الله [la illah illa allah] there is no other God but Allah

Political, people

أنور السادات [anwar e-sadat] Anwar Sadat, former President of Egypt

جمال عبد الناصر [gamāl *abd e-nassir] Gamal Abdel Nasser

الرئيس حسني مبارك [e-ra'ees Hosnee moobaaruhk] President Hosny Mubarak

الحزب الوطني الديمقراطي [el Hezb el wotuhnee e-deemokraatee] The National Democratic Party

Places, buildings

السد العالي [e-sadd el *alee] Aswan Dam

الجامع الأزرق *[el gāmi*a el azra']*
The Blue Mosque

برج القاهرة *[borg el kaheera]* Cairo Tower

جامعة القاهرة *[gama*it el kaheera]* Cairo University

حديقة الحيوانات *[Hadeekit el HIawaanet]* Cairo Zoo

المماليك *[el mamaleek]* City of the Dead (Tombs of the Mamelukes)

مسجد الحسين *[mazgid el Hossayn]* Hussein Mosque

جامع ابن طولون *[gāmi*a ibn tooloon]* Ibn Tulun Mosque

المتحف الإسلامي *[el matHaf el islāmee]* Islamic Museum

جامع الأزهر *[mazgid el uhz-huhr]* el Uzar mosque

جامع محمد علي *[gāmi*a moHamed *alee]* Mohamed Ali Mosque

جامع *[gāmi*a]* mosque

خان الخليلي *[khan el khaleelee]* oriental bazaars

الموسكى *[el muskee]* street of the oriental merchants

جامع السلطان حسن *[gāmi*a e-sultaan Hassan]* Sultan Hassan Mosque

الخليفة *[el khaleefa]* tombs of the Caliphs

Ancient Egypt

كليوباترا *[killee-obatra]* Cleopatra

ايزيس *[izees]* Isis

نفرتارى *['nefertari']* Nefertari

نفرتيتى *['nefertiti']* Nefertiti

الأهرام *[el ahraam]* The Pyramids

رمسيس *[ramsees]* Ramses

أبو الهول *[aboo el hol]* The Sphinx

معبد أبو سمبل *[ma*abad aboo simbil]* Temple of Abu Simbel

وادى الملوك *[wēdee el milook]* Valley of the Kings

CUSTOMS

جمارك *[gamarik]* customs

للأجانب فقط *[lil agēnib fakuht]* foreigners only

في حدود المسموح *[fee Hedood el masmooH]* nothing to declare

جوازات *[gawazēt]* passports

زيادة عن المسموح *[zeeyada *an el masmooH]* something to declare

DAYS OF THE WEEK

السبت *[yum e-sābt]* Saturday

الأحد *[yum el Had]* Sunday

الأثنين *[yum el itneen]* Monday

الثلاثاء *[yum e-talaat]* Tuesday

الأربعاء *[yum el arba*a]* Wednesday

الخميس *[yum el khamees]* Thursday

الجمعة [yum e-gom*a] Friday

أيام [Iyēm] days

DEPARTMENT STORE SECTIONS

بياضات [bIyadaat] bed linen

سجاد وموكيت [sigad wa mukitt] carpets

قسم الشباب [kism e-shebab] casual clothes

قسم الأطفال [kism el atfaal] childrens' department

ساعات وفضيات [sa*at wa fedeeyaat] clocks, watches and silver

أدوات تجميل [adawet tagmeel] cosmetics

أقطان [aktaan] cottons (fabric)

موبيليا [mobilya] furniture

روائح وهدايا [rawIyaH wa hadaya] gifts and perfumes

أدوات منزلية [adawet manzilaya] hardware

مجوهرات [moogow-haraat] jewel(le)ry

جاهز سيدات [gehiz sayeedat] ladies' fashions

لانجيرى [langeeree] lightweight fabrics

ملابس داخلية للسيدات [malabis dakhilaya lil sayeedat] lingerie

جاهز رجالي [gehiz rigālee] mens' fashions

أصواف رجالى [aswaaf rigālee] mens' tailoring fabrics in wool

راديو وتلفزيون [radyo wa televizyōn] radio and television

قمصان [umsaan] shirts

أحذية [aHzaya] shoes

حراير [Harrayuhr] silks

لعب أطفال [le*ab atfaal] toys and games

ديكور [dikor] wallpapers

DOCTORS *see* **MEDICAL**

DO NOT …

خطر [khattuhr] danger

خطر لا تلمس [khattuhr la talmis] dangerous, don't touch

ممنوع الجلوس على الخضرة [mamnoo-a* el giloos *ala el khodra] do not sit on the grass

لا تستعمل آلة التنبيه [la testa*mil elit e-tambee] do not sound your horn

ممنوع … [mamnoo-a* …] … forbidden

منطقة عسكرية

ممنوع الاقتراب والتصوير [muhntee'a *askaraya mamnoo-a* el ektirab wa e-tuhsweer] military zone, keep clear, no photography

ممنوع لعب الكرة [mamnoo-a* le*ab el kora] no ball games

ممنوع الاستحمام [mamnoo-a* el estiHmem] no bathing

ممنوع التخييم [mamnoo-a* e-takheem] no camping

ممنوع الدخول [mamnoo-a* e-dikhool] no entry

ممنوع الانتظار [mamnoo-a* el intizaar] no parking

ممنوع التصوير [mamnoo-a* e-tuhsweer] no photographs

ممنوع التدخين [mamnoo-a* e-tadkheen] no smoking

ممنوع الوقوف [mamnoo-a* el wokoof] no stopping

ممنوع السباحة [mamnoo-a* e-sibaHa] no swimming

ممنوع المرور [mamnoo-a* el muroor] no trespassing

DRINKS ON MENUS

سفن أب ['7 Up'] 7-Up (tm)

قهوة كابتشينو [ahwa 'cappuccino'] cappuccino coffee

خروب [kharoob] carob

كوكاكولا [kakōla] coca cola (tm)

كاكاو [kakow] cocoa

سبورت كولا ['sport cola'] diet coke (tm)

قهوة أكسبرسو [ahwa 'espresso'] espresso coffee

عصير موز [*aseer mooz] fresh banana milk shake

عصير جزر [*aseer guhzuhr] fresh carrot juice

عصير جوافة [*aseer guwafa] fresh guava juice

عصير ليمون [*aseer lamoon] fresh lemonade

عصير برتقال [*aseer bortookaan; spoken: *aseer bortoo'aan] fresh orange juice

عصير فراولة [*aseer farowla] fresh strawberry juice

عصير قصب [*aseer asuhb] fresh sugar cane juice

جرب فروت [graybfroot] grapefruit juice

حلبة [Helba] helba, drink made from boiled fenugreek seeds

كركدية [karkaday] hibiscus drink

بيرة ستلا [beera stella] lager

عرقسوس [*arkoosoos; spoken: *ar'oosoos] liquorice, licorice

عصير مانجو [*aseer manga] mango juice

مياه معدنية [meeyē ma*adanaya] mineral water

كوكتيل ['cocktail'] mixed fruit juices

كندا دراى ['canada dry'] mixers

تيم [teem (tm)] orange drink

بيبسى كولا ['pepsi'] pepsi (tm)

سحلب [saHlab] similar to Horlicks (tm)

صودا ['soda'] soda water

مشروب بيرل [mashroob birl] spa (spring) water

تمر هندى [tamr hindee] tamarind juice

شاى [shay] tea

قهوة [ahwa] Turkish coffee

EATING AND DRINKING PLACES

بار ['bar'] bar

بوفيه [buffay] café

نادى [nēdee] coffee and gaming house

كشرى [kōsharee] eat-in (or take-away) for 'kosharee', a typical Egyptian rice speciality

جروبى [grobbee] Groppi – the best ice cream parlour/parlor and patisserie in Cairo

عصير وفواكه [*aseer wa fawakih] juice bar

حاتى [Hattee] kebab house

فطاطرى [fataatree] pastry shop

حلوانى [Halawēnee] patisserie

كازينو ['casino'] picturesque tea room and bar, usually by the Nile

مطعم [mat*am] restaurant

كافيتريا ['cafeteria'] snack bar

فلفلة [filfilla] the best known restaurant for authentic Egyptian food

قهوة [ahwa] traditional coffee house

EMERGENCIES

الجمهورية [el gomhoraya] 24-hour pharmacy service

إسعاف [isa*af] ambulance

مطافى القاهرة [mataafee el kaheera] Cairo Fire Brigade/Department

مديرية أمن القاهرة [modarayit amn el kaheera] Cairo Police H.Q.

قسم الدقى [kism e-dokkee; spoken: e-do'ee] Dokki Police Station (opposite Sheraton Hotel, Cairo)

مخرج [makhruhg] emergency exit

حنفية حريق [Hanafayit Haree'] fire hydrant

قسم . . . [kism ...] police station for ... (name of area)

شرطة السكة الحديد [shortit e-sikka el Hadeed] Railway/ Railroad Police

شرطة السياحة [shortit e-seeyēHa] Tourist Police

EXCLAMATIONS AND SWEARWORDS

allah wa akbar! *God almighty!*

ela*na! *damn!*

ghebee! *fool!, idiot!*

hala hala! *well, well!, well I never!*

Hasib! *look out!*

inta*ama? *are you blind?*

mush teHasib? *can't you watch what you're doing?*

ya salēm! *my goodness! (literally: oh peace!)*

FOOD

Oriental hors d'oeuvres, Starters and side dishes

بابا غنوج [baba ghanoog] aubergine/eggplant purée

فول مدمس [fool midamis] brown bean purée, Egyptian national dish

تبولة [taboola] cracked wheat and tomato salad

طعمية [ta*amaya] fried balls of ground beans and herbs

سلطة خضراء [salata khadra] green salad

بذنجان مخلل [bitingan mikhallil] marinated aubergine/eggplant

سلطة شرقى [salata shar'ee] oriental (mixed vegetable) salad

حمص [Hommos] puréed chickpeas

طحينة [taHeena] sesame seed paste

سلطة بيضة [salata bayda] spiced yoghurt served with herbs

ورق عنب [warak *Inab; spoken: wara'] stuffed vine leaves

سلطة طماطم [saltit tomaatim] tomato salad

جبنة بيضاء بالطماطم [gibna bayda bi tomaatim] white cheese with tomato salad

Soups

شوربة فراخ [shorbit ferēkh] chicken soup

فتة [fata] feastday soup of meat stock from a sacrificial lamb, with bread, rice and tomato

شوربة عدس [shorbit *ads] lentil soup

شوربة لحمة [shorbit laHma] meat soup

ملوخية [molokhaya] traditional soup laden with garlic and made from a spinach-like Egyptian vegetable of the marrow family

شوربة خضار [shorbit khodaar] vegetable soup

Egg dishes

عجة [*Iga] baked omelet(te) with onion

بيض مسلوق [bayd masloo'] boiled eggs

بيض مقلى [bayd ma'allee] fried eggs

Food

أومليت *['omelette']* omelet(te)

بيض بكبدة فراخ *[bayd bi kibdit ferekh]* scrambled eggs with chopped chicken liver

بيض بسطرمة *[bayd basterma]* scrambled eggs with cold meat

شكشوكة *[shakshooka; spoken: sha'shoo'a]* scrambled eggs with mince/ground beef

Meat and meat dishes

مخ *[mokh]* brains

لحمة كندوز *[laHma kandooz]* braising meat

فراخ *[ferēkh]* chicken

بط *[buht]* duck

لحم فلتو *[laHm flittoo]* fillet mignon

وز *[wizz]* goose

مشويات متنوعة *[mashweeyēt]* grills

نصف فرخة مشوية *[nus ferkha mashwaya]* half a grilled chicken

شيش كباب وكفتة *[sheesh kebab wi kofta]* kebabs with meatballs

لحم ضانى بريانى *[laHm daanee 'biryani']* lamb biryani

كبدة *[kibda]* liver

لحمة بتلو *[laHma bi telloo]* meat on the bone

لحمة ضانى *[laHma daanee]* mutton

حمام *[Hammem]* pigeon

أرانب *[arānib]* rabbit

سجق *[soogo']* similar to haggis

شاورمة *[shawerma]* slices of spit-roast lamb

لحمة أوزى *[laHma oozee]* spring lamb

ريش لحم بقرى *[reesh laHm ba'ree]* steak on the bone

حمام محشى *[Hammem maHshee]* stuffed pigeon

ديك رومي *[deek roomee]* turkey

اسكالوب بتلو *['escaloppe' bi telloo]* veal escalope

Vegetarian dishes

كرنب محشى *[kuromb maHshee]* stuffed cabbage

كوسة محشية *[kosa maHshaya]* stuffed courgettes/zucchinis

فلفل محشى *[filfil maHshee]* stuffed peppers

بطاطس محشية *[bataatis maHshaya]* stuffed potatoes

طاجن خضار *[taagin khodaar]* vegetables baked with tomatoes

Rice, pulses, pasta

كشرى *[kōsharee]* a mixture of rice, lentils, macaroni and onions with a hot tomato sauce

لوبيا *[lobia]* beans (*small black-eyed*)

فول *[fool]* brown Egyptian beans

حمص [Hommos] chickpeas

فريك [fireek] cracked wheat

طعمية [ta*amaya] deep-fried balls of spiced bean purée

فاصوليا [fasolia] haricot beans

عدس بجبة [*ads (bigebba)] lentils (small brown)

مكرونة [makarōna] macaroni

شعرية [sha*raya] noodles, vermicelli

عدس أصفر [*ads (asfar)] orange lentils

فول مدمس [fool midamis] puréed brown Egyptian beans

رز [ruz] rice

رز بشعرية [ruz bi sha*raya] rice with noodles

مكرونة عيدان [makarōna *Idan] spaghetti

Fish and fish dishes

طاجن سمك [taagin samak] baked fish

قراميط [arameet] catfish

كابوريا [kaboree-a] crab

تعابين [ta*abeen] eels

ترنشات [taranshaat] fillets

. . . مقلى [... ma'allee] fried ...

. . . مشوى [... mashwee] grilled ...

. . . بزيت [... bi zayt] ... in oil

بورى [booree] mullet

طاجن جمبرى [taagin gambaree] potted shrimps

جمبرى [gambaree] prawns

أرز بالجمبرى [ruz bi gambaree] prawns and rice

رنجة [ringuh] salted fish

سردين ['sardine'] sardines

مكرونة [makarōna] type of fish

بلطى [boltee] type of freshwater fish

مرجان [morgan] type of freshwater fish

Types of bread

عيش [*I-esh] bread

فينو مدور [feeno medowar] bread rolls

عيش بلدى [*I-esh baladee] round, flat, rough wholemeal

عيش شامى [*I-esh shāmee] round, flat, white pitta-type bread

سندوتش ['sandwich'] sandwich

سميط [simeet] sesame-crusted bread rings

فينو [feenō] whitish baguette (French loaf)

Vegetables

خرشوف [kharshoof] artichokes

بتنجان [bitingan] aubergines, eggplants

فول حيراتى [fool Heraatee] broad beans

كرنب [kuromb] cabbage

جزر [guhzuhr] carrots

قرنبيط [arnabeet] cauliflower

فلفل حامى [filfil Hāmee] chillies

كوسة [kosa] courgettes, zucchinis

آته [ata] cucumber (large)

خيار [kheeyar] cucumber (small)

توم [tom] garlic

فاصوليا [fasolia] green beans

فلفل أخضر [filfil akhdar] green peppers

خس [khass] lettuce

نعناع [ne*ana*] mint

بامية [bamya] okra, ladies' fingers

بصل [basal] onions

بقدونس [ba'doonis] parsley

بسلة [bisilluh] peas

بطاطس [bataatis] potatoes

سبانخ [sabenekh] spinach, beet

بصل أخضر [basal akhdar] spring onions

ذوره [dora] sweet corn, maize

بطاطا [bataataa] sweet potatoes

طماطم [oota] tomatoes

لفت [lift] turnips

ورق عنب [wara' *Inab] vine leaves

جرجير [guhrgir] watercress

فجل [figl] white radish

Fruit and nuts

لوز [loz] almonds

تفاح [tufē-aH] apples

مشمش [mishmish] apricots

موز [mooz] bananas

جوز الهند [gooz el hind] coconut

بلح [balaH] dates

تين [teen] figs

عنب [*Inab] grapes (large, sweet and yellow)

عنب بناتى [*Inab banatee] grapes (small and seedless)

جوافة [gawafa] guava

بندق [bundo'] hazelnuts

ليمون أصفر [lamoon (asfar)] lemons

ليمون [lamoon] limes

مانجة [manga] mango

شمام [shamēm] melon

توت [toot] mulberries

برتقال بسرة [bortoo'aan bisora] oranges (of the large navel kind)

خوخ [khokh] peaches

فول سوداني [fool sudanee] peanuts

كمثرى [komitruh] pears

حمص [Hommos] peas (small and roasted)

أناناس *[ananas]* pineapple

فستق *[fozdo']* pistachio nuts

رومان *[romaan]* pomegranates

لب *[lib]* roasted seeds (of melon, sunflower etc)

يوسفى *[ostafendee]* satsumas

فراولة *[farowla]* strawberries

عين جمل *[*in gamal]* walnuts

بطيخ *[bateekh]* water melon

برقوق *[barkook; spoken: bar'oo']* plums

برتقال *[bortookaan; spoken: bortoo'aan]* oranges

Cakes, sweets and desserts

جلاش *[gulesh]* baklawa – fine layers of pastry and nuts soaked in syrup

بسبوسة *[basboosa]* cake made with semolina and soaked in syrup

خشاف *[khoshēf]* compote of stewed fruits eaten during Ramadan

زلابية *[zalabiya]* fritters soaked in syrup

فروت سلاط *['fruit salad']* fruit salad

مهلبية *[mahalabaya]* ground rice with milk and rosewater

آيس كريم *['ice cream']* ice cream

بلوظة *[balooza]* milk pudding made with cornflour

قطايف *[attf]* pancake, thick and stuffed with nuts

أرز باللبن *[ruz bi laban]* rice pudding

كنافة *[kunafa]* sticky pastry with nuts and syrup

أم على *[um *alee]* traditional pudding made with raisins, cake and milk

Basics

بسكويت *[baskaweet]* biscuits, cookies

زبدة *[zebda]* butter

جبنة *[gibna]* cheese

سمنة *[samna]* clarified butter

قهوة *[ahwa]* coffee

بيض *[bayd]* eggs

دقيق *[di'ee']* flour

عسل نحل *[*asal naHl]* honey

مربة *[mirabuh]* jam

لبن *[laban]* milk

عسل اسود *[*asal eswid]* molasses

زيت *[zayt]* oil

زيت زيتون *[zayt zetoon]* olive oil

فلفل أسود *[filfil eswid]* pepper

ملح *[malH]* salt

سكر *[sukar]* sugar

شای *[shay]* tea

خل *[khel]* vinegar

زبادی *[zabēdee]* yoghurt

Cheeses

جبنة رومی *[gibna roomee]* hard cheese

جبنة نستو *[gibna nistoo]* processed cheese wedges

جبنة بيضة *[gibna bayda]* salty white cheese

جبنة فلاحی *[gibna fellaHee]* similar to cottage cheese

جبنة قديمة *[gibna adeema]* strongly matured 'g*ibna fellaHee*'

جبنة تلاجة *[gibna talēga]* very mild white cheese

FOOD LABELS

المحتويات *[el moHtawayēt]* contents

تاريخ الانتاج *[tareekh el intag]* date of manufacture

الوزن الصافی *[el wazn e-saafee]* net weight

السعر للمستهلك *[e-se*ar lil mustahlik]* price

بروتينات *[brōteenēt]* protein

تاريخ الانتهاء *[tareekh el intiha']* sell-by date

سكريات *[sukareeyēt]* sugar

مدة الصلاحية *[modit e-salaHaya ...]* will keep for ...

فيتامينات *[vitameenēt]* vitamins

FORMS

العنوان address

العنوان فی مصر address in Egypt

التاريخ date

تاريخ الميلاد date of birth

تاريخ الإصدار date of issue

مدة الاقامة duration of stay

الاسم بالكامل full name

الجنسية nationality

المهنة occupation

رقم جواز السفر passport number

جهة الميلاد place of birth

جهة الإصدار place of issue

الديانة religion

توقيع signature

رقم التأشيرة visa number

GARAGES

هواء *[howa]* air

خدمة الغسيل الآلی *[khedmit el gheseel el alee]* automatic car wash

موقف سيارات *[mow'af styaraat]* car park, parking lot

فرش ودواسات السيارات *[farsh wa dawāset e-styaraat]* car upholstery sales

الدخول ببطء *[e-dikhool bee bot']* enter slowly

بيع وأصلاح اطارات [be*a wa islaaH etaaraat] full tyre/tire service

هدايا ولعب أطفال [hadaya wa le*ab atfaal] gifts and children's games

الخروج ببطء [el khuroog bee bot'] leave slowly

تشحيم وتغيير زيت [tashHeem wi tagheer zayt] lubrication and oil change

موبيل [mobil] mobil (tm)

ممنوع التدخين [mamnoo-a* e-tadkheen] no smoking

غسيل راديتير [gheseel 'radiator'] radiator water change

بنزين مخصوص [benzeen makhsoos] special grade petrol/gas

بنزين سوبر ٨٠ [benzeen 'super 80'] super 80 petrol/gas

بنزين سوبر ٩٠ [benzeen 'super 90'] super 90 petrol/gas

اطارات وبطاريات [etaaraat wa battareeyaat] tyres/tires and batteries

جراج ['garage'] underground parking

ضبط زوايا واتزان [duhbt zawaya wa etizan] wheel balancing

GEOGRAPHICAL

حدود [Hedood] border

قناة [koneh] canal

دلتا [deltuh] delta

صحراء [saHra] desert

قسم [markaz] district

شرق [shar'] east

محافظة [moHafzuh] governorate, administrative district

خليج [khaleeg] gulf

جزيرة [gezeeruh] island

بركة [birka] lake

جبل [gabal] mount

شمال [shimēl] north

واحة [weHa] oasis

راس [ras] point, head

مديرية [modoraya] province

نهر [nahr] river

ملاحة [malēHa] salt lake

جنوب [ganoob] south

عين [*In] spring

وادى [wēdee] valley

غرب [gharb] west

GREETINGS see **REPLIES**

HAIRDRESSERS

كوافير . . . [kowafayar] ladies' hairdresser

صالون . . . [salōn ...] ... salon

HOSPITALS see **MEDICAL**

HOTELS

بنسيون [benseeyōn] boarding house

الخزينة [el khazeena] cashier

فندق [fondō'] hotel

الاستعلامات [el ista*lamat] information

الاستقبال [el isti'bel] reception

لوكاندة [lokanduh] small hotel

دورة المياه [dowrit el meeyē] toilet, rest room

MEDICAL

قسم استقبال الحوادث [kism isti'bel el Howādis] casualty department

عيادة [*Iyāda] clinic

جراح أسنان [garaH asnan] dentist

اخصائي أمراض جلدية [akhissaa'ee uhmraad gildaya] dermatologist

دكتور ... [doktor ...] Dr ...

جراح أنف وأذن وحنجرة [garaH ozuhn wa anf wa Hungara] ear, nose and throat specialist

جراح عيون [garaH *Iyoon] eye specialist

أخصائي أمراض القلب [akhissaa'ee uhmraad el alb] heart specialist

مستشفى [mustashfa] hospital

أخصائي ولادة وأمراض نساء [akhissaa'ee wilāda wa uhmraad nissa] obstetrician and gyn(a)ecologist

أخصائي بصريات [akhissaa'ee basareeyaat] optician

جراح عظام [garaH *Izaam] orthop(a)edic doctor

أخصائي عظام [akhissaa'ee *Izaam] orthop(a)edic specialist

قسم العيادة الخارجية [kism el *Iyēda el kherigaya] out-patients

MEDICINE LABELS

للبالغين adults

حقن ampoules

حسب ارشادات الطبيب as directed by the physician

متوسط الجرعة اليومية average daily dose

كبسولات capsules

للأطفال الكبار children

التركيب composition

الجرعة dose/dosage

الأثر الطبى indications

للأطفال الرضع infants

مجم mg

سم ٣ ml

قرص ٣ مرات يوميا one tablet three times daily

ملعقة صغيرة كل ٤ أو ٦ ساعات

يومياً one teaspoonful every
   4-6 hours

الأثار الجانبية side effects

معلق suspension

أقراص tablets

ملعقة صغيرة teaspoonful

MEN'S NAMES

عبد الـ . . . Abdel ...

أبو Abu

عادل Adel

أحمد Ahmed

علي Ali

أشرف Ashraf

عاصم Assam

عاطف Atef

جمال Gamal

حسن Hassan

حسين Hussein

إبراهيم Ibrahim

خالد Khaled

محمود Mahmood

منصور Mansoor

محمد Mohamed

محسن Mohsen

مختار Mokhtar

مصطفى Mustapha

نبيل Nabil

ناصر Nasser

عمر Omar

صلاح Salah

صالح Saleh

سمير Samir

سيد Sayeed

طاهر Taher

MONTHS OF THE YEAR

يناير *[yanaayuhr]* January

فبراير *[fibrɪuhr]* February

مارس *[mēris]* March

أبريل *[abreel]* April

مايو *[mayoo]* May

يونيو *[yoonyoo; spoken: yoonya]*
   June

يوليو *[yulyoo; spoken: yulya]* July

أغسطس *[aghostos]* August

سبتمبر *[sibtimbuhr]* September

أكتوبر *[oktōbuhr]* October

نوفمبر *[novimbuhr]* November

ديسمبر *[disimbuhr]* December

شهور *[shuhor]* months

MOVIE THEATERS *see* **CINEMAS**

MUSICIANS, SINGERS

عبد الحليم Abdel Haleem

عبد الوهاب Abdel Wahebb

فريد الأطرش Fareed el Atruhsh

فيروز Fayrooz

أم كلثوم Um Khalsoom

وردة Warda

NIGHT SPOTS

بار ['bar'] bar

كازينو ['casino'] bar in romantic spot along the Nile

كابريه ['cabaret'] cabaret

ملهى ليلى [malha laylee] night club

صحارى سيتى ['sahara city'] night club in a tent in the desert outside Cairo with the most varied floorshow of traditional dancing

NOTICES IN RESTAURANTS, BARS AND ON MENUS

١٠٪ خدمة [10% khedma] 10% service charge

مشروبات [mashroobaat] drinks

أطباق البيض [uhtbaa' el bayd] egg dishes

مشويات [mashweeyēt] grills

أطباق شرقية [uhtbaa' shar'aya] oriental dishes

نشويات [nashweeyēt] rice and pastas

أنواع الشرب [anwa* e-shoruhb] soups

حلويات [Halaweeyēt] sweets, desserts

الأسعار شاملة الخدمة والضريبة [el as*ar shamla el khedma wa e-dareeba] taxes and services included

الادارة ترحب بكم دائماً [el idaara tooraHib bikum dayimman] the management welcomes you

دورة المياه [dowrit el meeyē] toilet, rest room

NOTICES IN SHOPS

خزينة [khazeena] cashier

كنترول ['control'] goods collection point

البضاعة المباعة لا ترد ولا تستبدل [el beda*a el mobe*a la tooruhd walla tustabdel] no exchange or refund

أسعارنا في متناول الجميع [as*aruhnna fee mutanawil e-gamee*a] our prices are modest

مدير الفرع [modeer el farra*] store manager

الزبون دائماً على حق [e-ziboon dayimman *ala Hak] the customer is always right

دورة المياه [dowrite el meeyē] toilet, rest room

شيكات سياحية للبيع هنا [sheekat seeyaHaya lil bay*a hena] traveller's cheques/traveler's checks sold here

NOTICES ON DOORS AND GATES

هواء مكيف [howa' mookayif]
air-conditioned

مغلق [moghluhk] closed

العطلة الأسبوعية [el *otla el
isboo-*ıya] closing days

دخول [dikhool] entrance

خروج [khuroog] exit

من . . . إلى . . . [min ... illa ...]
from ... to ...

المدير [el modeer] manager's office

ممنوع الدخول [mamnoo-a*
e-dikhool] no entry

ممنوع الوقوف امام البوابة
[mamnoo-a* el wookoof amam el
bewaba] no parking in front of
these gates

مفتوح [maftooH] open

مواعيد العمل [mowa*ıd el *amal]
opening hours

اسحب [esHab] pull

ادفع [edfa*] push

مرحبا [marHabban] welcome

PLACE NAMES

العباسية [el *abbasaya] Abbasiya

عابدين [*abdeen] Abdin

أبو سمبل [aboo simbil] Abu Simbel

العجوزة [el *agooza] Aguza

الاسكندرية [el iskindraya]

Alexandria

أسيوط [assyoot] Assyut

أسوان [aswaan] Aswan

ميدان العتبة [midan el *ataba]
Ataba Square

باب الخلق [bab el khal'] Bab
el Khalq

باب اللوق [babelook; spoken:
babeloo'] Bab el Ook

باب زويلة [bab ziwayla]
Bab Zuwaila

بنى سويف [benee swayf] Beni Suef

القاهرة [el kaheera] Cairo

القلعة [el al*a] Citadel

دهب [dahab] Dahab

دهشور [dahshur] Dashur

الدقى [e-dokkee; spoken: e-do'ee]
Dokki

إدفو [edfoo] Edfu

البدرشين [el badrasheen] El
Badrshein

الفيوم [el fayoom] El Faiyum

الخارجة [el kharga] El Kharga

المنصورة [el mansoora] El Mansura

المنيا [el minya) El Minya

الموسكى [el muskee] El Muski

السيدة زينب [e-sayeda zaynab]
El Saiyida Zeinab

إسنا [esna] Esna

جاردن سیتی [*'garden city'*]
Garden City

الجيزة [*el geezuh*] Giza

دير البحارى [*dē-ir el baHaree*]
Hatshepsut's temple

مصر الجديدة [*masr el gedeeda*]
Heliopolis

حلوان [*Helwān*] Helwan

إمبابة [*imbaba*] Imbaba

الاسماعيلية [*el isma*laya*] Ismailia

الكرنك [*el karnak*] Karnak

مرسى مطروح [*marsa matrooH*]
Marsa Matruh

المقطم [*el Mokattam; spoken:*
el mo'attam] Mokattam

مدينة نصر [*medeenit nasr*] Nasser
City

القرنة الجديدة [*el gurna e-gedeeda*]
New Gurna

مصر القديمة [*masr el adeema*]
Old Cairo

القرنة القديمة [*el gurna el adeema*]
Old Gurna

بورسعيد [*bor sa*yeed*] Port Said

قنا [*kenna; spoken: enna*] Kena

خان الخليلي [*khan el khaleelee*]
Khan el Khalili

كوم أمبو [*komumboo*] Kom Ombo

ميدان التحرير [*midan e-taHreer*]
Liberation Square

الأقصر [*el lu'sor*] Luxor

المعادى [*el ma*adee*] Maadi

المنيل [*el manyal*] Manial or Geziret
el Roda

ميدان رمسيس [*midan ramsees*]
Ramses Square

سقارة [*Sakkara; spoken: sa'ara*]
Sakkara

شرم الشيخ [*sharuhm e-shekh*)
Sharm el Sheikh

سينا [*seena*] Sinai

سيوة [*seewa*] Siwa

سوهاج [*soohag*] Sohag

السويس [*el Soo-is*] Suez

طنطا [*tuhntuh*] Tante

مدينة هابو [*medeenit haboo*]
temples of Ramses

وادى الملوك [*wēdee el milook*]
Valley of the Kings

وادى الملكات [*wēdee el maleekat*]
Valley of the Queens

وادى حوف [*wēdee Hof*]
Wadi Halfa

زمالك [*zamalik*] Zamalik

POST OFFICE

بريد جوى [*bareed gawee*] airmail

مستعجل [*mista*gil*] express

قابل للكسر [*kaabil lil kasr*] fragile

خطابات داخلية *[khitabaat dakhilaya]* inland mail

صندوق بريد *[sandoo' bareed]* letterbox

خطابات *[khitabaat]* letters

عادى *[*adee]* ordinary

عادى ١٠ جرام الدول العربية *[el *arabaya *adee e-diwil]* rate for 10g to other Arab countries

بيع الطوابع *[be*a e-tawaabe*a]* postage stamps

رسوم التخليص *[risoom e-taakhlees]* postal charges

مكتب بريد *[maktab bareed]* post office

عادى ١٠ جرام الدول الأجنبية *[*adee e-diwil el agnabaya]* rate for 10g to non-Arab countries

خطابات خارجية *[khitabaat kherigaya]* overseas mail

مستعجل ٢٠ جرام *[mista*gil]* rate for 20g express service

عادى ٢٠ جرام *[*adee]* rate for 20g inland mail

PUBLIC BUILDINGS

جامعة عين شمس *[gama*it *In shams]* Ain Shams University

المعهد البريطاني *[el ma*had el britaanee]* British Council

محافظة القاهرة *[moHuhfzit el kaheera]* Cairo Governorate HQ

متحف الآثار *[matHaf el asaar]* Cairo Museum of Antiquities

متحف البريد *[matHaf el bareed]* Cairo Postal Museum

القصر العيني *[el asr el *Ianee]* Cairo University Medical School

قنصلية ... *[konsulayit ...]* Consulate of ...

سفارة ... *[safaarit ...]* Embassy of ...

كلية ... *[kullayit ...]* faculty of ...

المجمع *[el mogamma]* Government Central Department of Information (*Cairo*)

مستشفى ... *[mustashfa ...]* ... Hospital

مكتبة *[maktaba]* library

وزارة ... *[wizaarit ...]* Ministry of ...

وزارة الزراعة *[wizaarit e-zira*a]* Ministry of Agriculture

وزارة السياحة *[wizaarit e-seeyēHa]* Ministry of Tourism

متحف ... *[matHaf ...]* museum of ...

مكتب تلغراف وتليفون *[maktab teleghraaf wa telefōn]* Office for Telegraphs and Telephones

قسم ... *[kism ...]* ... Police

Station

مبنى الأذاعة والتلفزيون *[mabna el iza*a wa e-televizyōn]* Radio and Television Building (*Cairo*)

محطة . . . *[maHattit …]* … railway station, … train station

مدرسة . . . *[madrassit …]* … school

PUBLIC HOLIDAYS (EGYPTIAN)

عيد تحرير سيناء *[*Iyeed taHreer seena]* Sinai Liberation Day (*April 25th*)

عيد العمال *[*Iyeed el *omēl]* Labour/Labor Day (*May 1st*)

عيد الثورة *[*Iyeed e-sowra]* Anniversary of the Revolution (*July 23rd*)

عيد القوات المسلحة ـ عيد ٦ أكتوبر *[*Iyeed el koowat el musalaHa]* Armed Forces Day (*Oct 6th*)

عيد النصر *[*Iyeed e-nuhsr]* Victory Day (*Dec 23rd*)

عيد الأضحى *[*Iyeed el uhdHa; spoken: el *Iyeed e-kebeer]* Big Feast

رأس السنة الهجرية *[raas e-sana el hegraya]* Islamic New Year

المولد النبوى الشريف *[el mowlid e-nabowee e-shereef]* Mohamed's birthday

عيد الفطر *[*Iyeed el fitr; spoken: el *Iyeed e-sooghIyar]* Small Feast

شم النسيم *[sham e-nesseem]* Spring Celebration

RAILWAY STATION

حجز تذاكر . . . *[Hagz tazēkir …]* advance booking for …

استراحة *[istiraHa]* buffet

محطة مصر *[maHattit masr]* Cairo Main Railway/Railroad Station

هيئة سكك حديد مصر *[hI'it sikkuhk Hadeed masr]* Egypt Railways/Railroad

درجة أولى . . . *[… daraga oola]* first class

اسعاف محطة القاهرة *[is*af maHattit el kaheera]* first aid post

معلومات *[ma*loomēt]* information

امانات *[amanēt]* left luggage, baggage checkroom

رصيف . . . *[raseef …]* platform no. …, track no. …

درجة ثانية . . . *[… daraga tania]* second class

درجة ثالثة . . . *[… daraga talta]* third class

شباك تذاكر . . . *[shebek tazēkir]* ticket office

تذاكر *[tazēkir]* tickets

REPLIES

shukran *thank you*

*afwan *not at all, don't mention it*

el *afw *not at all, don't mention it*

sabaH el kheer *good morning*

sabaH e-noor *good morning* (*reply*)

misē' el kheer *good evening*

misē' e-noor *good evening* (*reply*)

salemmoo *aleekum *hello*

*aleekum e-salēm *hello* (*reply*)

izzayak? (*to man*); izzayik? (*to woman*) *how are you?*

kwɪyis (*said by man*); kwɪyissa (*said by woman*) *I'm fine*

el Hamdu lillah *I'm fine* (*literally – thanks be to God*)

wa inta? (*to man*); wa intee? (*to woman*) *and you?*

ahlan *welcome*

ahlan wa sahlan *nice to meet you*

asif *sorry*

ba*dak (*to man*); ba*dik (*to woman*) *after you*

Haraam *aleek! *that's very wrong, forbidden*

in sha' allah *God willing*

itfuhduhl (*to man*); itfuhduhlee (*to woman*) *come in; help yourself etc* (*literally – accept!*)

IwA *yes*

la' *no*

lowsamaHt *excuse me; please*

ma*alesh *never mind, it doesn't matter*

ma*a e-salemma *goodbye*

mabrook! *well done!, congratulations!*

mafeesh *there isn't any*

na*am *yes*

salamtak (*to man*); salamtik (*to woman*) *get well soon, I hope you feel better soon*

RESTAURANTS *see* NOTICES IN RESTAURANTS

REST ROOMS *see* TOILETS

ROAD SIGNS

مركز اسعاف ونجدة ambulance station

طريق متعرج bendy road

انتبه caution

نص المدينة city centre/center

خطر ممنوع الأنتظار dangerous: no parking

منحنيان عموديان الأول على اليمين double right hand bends ahead

ورشة garage

أولوية المرور في الميدان للقادم من

give priority to traffic from يمينك
the right

keep to the right الزم اليمين

left turn الدوران للخلف شمالا
only

main road طريق رئيسى

maximum height أقصى أرتفاع ٤م
4m

maximum width أقصى عرض ٣م
3m

narrow bridge كوبرى ضيق

no lorries/trucks ممنوع مرور النقل

no traffic ممنوع السير من الجهتين
at all

ممنوع الانتظار بين اليافطتين
no waiting between the two signs

October 6th كوبرى ٦ اكتوبر
Bridge

park الانتظار موازى للرصيف
parallel to the pavement

private car موقف خصوصى
park/parking lot

مزلقان سكك حديد
railway/railroad crossing

railway/railroad مزلقان مقفول
crossing with barriers

reduce speed now هدى السرعة

right hand bend منحنى على اليمين

road منحنيات الأول على اليمين
bends first to the right

road dips مطب

school مدرسة

٦٠ كم /ساعة speed limit 60 km/h

steep hill منحدر خطر

STOP قف

stop at امامك علامة قف
junction/intersection

قف . . التفتيش بعد ٣٠٠ متر
traffic control ahead

traffic in this السير في هذا الاتجاه
direction

unguarded مزلقان مفتوح
railway/railroad crossing

ممنوع مرور السيارات التى يزيد
unladen وزنها على طنا
weight limit

ممنوع مرور السيارات التى تحمل
weight اكثر من طنا ٥ , ٥ طن
limit 5·5 tons

SCHEDULES *see* **TIMETABLES**

SHOP NAMES

[makhbaz] bakery مخبز

[salōn tagmeel] صالون تجميل
beauty salon

[maktaba] مكتبة
bookshop/bookstore and
stationery

[gizaarit ...] butcher جزارة

[agzakhenna] chemist, أجزاخانة
pharmacy

صيدلية [sIduhlaya] chemist, pharmacy

تحميض الأفلام الملونة [taHmeed el aflam el milowana] colo(u)r film processing

حلواني [Halawēnee] confectionery

ألبان [albān] dairy

مصبغة [muhsbuhgha] dry-cleaner

بقالة [bikaalit ...] groceries

فطاطري [fataatree] pastry shop/store

تصوير مستندات [tuhsweer mustanadet] photocopying

ستوديو [istudyo] photographer's studio

سوبر ماركت ['supermarket'] supermarket

STREETS

سكة [sikka] alley

كورنيش ['corniche'] corniche

زقاق [zoo'e'] cul-de-sac

عطفة [*atfa] lane

حارة [Haara] lane, alley

طريق [taree'] road

ميدان [midan] square

شارع [shāri*a] street

TAXIS

الأجرة [el ōgra] fare

أجرة [ōgra] for hire

حجز الليموزين [Hagz el 'limosine'] limousine service

تاكسى ['taxi'] taxi

موقف سيارات أجره [mow'af sIyaraat ōgra] taxi rank, taxi stand

TELEPHONES

سعر المكالمة [se*ar el mokalma] call charge

سعر الدقيقة بالقرش [se*ar e-duhkeeka bil kuhrsh] charge per minute in piastres

رقم الكود [rakuhm el 'code'] code number

دليل تليفونات تجارى [daleel telefonēt togaree] commercial telephone directory

مباشر للمحافظات [mobāshir lil moHafuhzaat] direct dial to other districts

دولى [dowlee] international

تليفون [telefōn] telephone

دليل تليفونات [daleel telefonēt] telephone directory

THEATRES, THEATERS

حجز تذاكر [Hagz tazēkir] advance bookings

كرسى بلكون [korsee balakōn] balcony seat

مسرح البالون [masraH el balloon] Balloon Theatre/Theater

(*Agooza*)

tape-recorders is prohibited

شباك تذاكر [*shebek tazēkir*] box office

مسرح . . . [*masraH ...*] ... theatre/theater

مخرج [*makhruhg*] exit

TIMETABLES, SCHEDULES

السيرك القومى [*e-sirk el kowmee*] National Circus (*Agooza*)

ق	س	hours	minutes
٧	٣٠	7	30

المسرح القومى [*el masraH el kowmee*] National Theatre/ Theater (*Ataba*)

ميعاد الوصول [*mee*ad el wisool*] arrival time

مسرح العرائس [*masraH el *ara'is*] Puppet Theatre/Theater (*Ataba*)

درجات [*daragaat*] class

يرفع الستار ٩ مساء [*yorfa* e-sittar 9 misē' en*] performance begins at 9 p.m.

نوع القطار [*no*a el kitaar*] class of train

أسعار الدخول [*as*ar e-dikhool*] price of admission

وقت القيام [*wokt el keeyēm*] departure time

البرنامج [*el birnāmig*] program(me)

ميعاد القيام [*mee*ad el keeyēm*] departure time

قاعة سيد درويش [*ka*aIt sayyeed daroo-eesh*] Sayyeed Daroo-eesh Concert Hall for Classical Arabic music

اكسبريس ['*express*'] express train

سياحى [*seeyēHee*] fast train with limited stops

كرسى فوتيل [*korsee footayl*] seat in box

مجرى [*magaree*] fast train with limited stops

كرسى ممتاز [*korsee momtaz*] seat in circle

درجة أولى [*daraga oola*] first class

ساعة [*sa*a*] hours

كرسى صالة [*korsee saala*] seat in stalls

دقيقة [*dikeeka; spoken: di'ee'a*] minutes

لوكس [*luks*] pullman train

ممنوع اصتحاب الكاميرات وأجهزة التسجيل [*mamnoo-a* estiHaab el kamiraat wa ag-hezzit e-tazgeel*] the use of cameras and

درجة ثانية [*daraga tania*] second class

جهة الوصول [*gehat el wisool*] terminates at ...

جدول المواعيد *[gadwil el mowa*ıd]*
timetable, schedule

رقم القطار *[rakuhm el kitaar]* train
number

TOILETS, REST ROOMS

للرجال *[lil rigāl]* gents, mens' rest
rooms

للسيدات *[lil sıyeedat]* ladies, ladies'
rest rooms

دورة المياه *[dowrit el meeyē]* toilet,
rest room

دورات المياه *[dawaraat el meeyē]*
toilets, rest rooms

TOURISM

حجز تذاكر ، طيران ـ بواخر
*[Hagz tazēkir tıyaraan wa
bawakhir]* advance booking for
air and sea travel

تأجير سيارات وأتوبيسات فاخرة
ومكيفة *[tageer sıyaraat wa
ōtōbeeset fakheera wa mokıyefa]*
car and bus rental service

رحلات يومية *[reHalat yomaya]* day
trips

حجز فنادق *[Hagz fanādi']* hotel
reservations

رحلات نيلية *[reHalat neelaya]* Nile
Cruises

رحلات سياحية *[reHalat
seeyaHaya]* package tours

YOUTH HOSTEL

بيت الشباب *[bayt e-shebab]* Youth
Hostel

Reference Grammar

NOUNS

GENDER

Nouns in Arabic are either masculine or feminine. Feminine nouns are the easier to identify and can be divided into the following groups:

1. Most nouns ending in **-a**:

нaga	thing
shanta	bag

Nouns which form an exception to this rule (masculine nouns ending in **-a**) are indicated in the English-Arabic section of this book, for example:

dowa	medicine (*m*)

2. Some basically masculine nouns, often relating to professions, which have been extended to feminine use by the addition of the final **-a**:

doktor (*m*)	**doktora** (*f*)	doctor
garson (*m*)	**garsona** (*f*)	waiter/waitress

3. Nouns relating to something obviously feminine:

bint	girl
um	mother

4. Names of many countries and cities:

masr	Egypt
kaheera	Cairo

5. Names of many parts of the body:

ras	head
rigl	leg

These will be marked as feminine in the text.

6. There is a final (random) group of nouns which are unpredictably feminine. These will all be marked in the text. Some examples are:

shams	sun
feloos	money
da'n	beard

You can assume that all other nouns are masculine.

CONSTRUCT FORM

Some rules require the final **-a** of a feminine noun to be replaced by **-it**, for example, when two nouns are used together:

foota	towel
Hammem	bath
footit el нammem	bath towel

PLURALS

There are three kinds of plurals in Arabic. They describe:

  (a) two of anything
  (b) three or more of anything
  (c) collective groups of things

(a) *the dual plural*

This is formed by the addition of suffixes to the singular form.

For masculine nouns and irregular feminine nouns (not ending in **-a**) add **-ayn**, for example:

sing.		dual plural	
walad	boy	**waladayn**	two boys
eed	hand	**eedayn**	(two) hands

Feminine nouns ending in **-a** usually lose the final **-a** and then add **-tayn**, for example:

sing.		dual plural	
ezaza	bottle	**ezaztayn**	two bottles
kubbaya	cup	**kubbaytayn**	two cups
нaga	thing	**нagtayn**	two things

There are two variations to this rule. Some nouns do not lose the final **-a**, for example:

mara	one time, once
maratayn	two times, twice

And some nouns add **-ayn** to the construct form (see page 99):

shirka	company
shirkitayn	two companies
shanta	bag
shantitayn	two bags

(b) *the standard plural*

This is also formed by adding suffixes to the singular noun.

For masculine nouns add **-een**, for example:

fellaн	peasant farmer
fellaнeen	peasant farmers

For feminine nouns add **-at**, for example:

*agala	bicycle
*agalaat	bicycles

In the English-Arabic section of this book you will see the pronunciation of the feminine plural given variously as **-et**, **-at**, **-aat**, depending on the actual sound of a particular word, for example:

ōtōbeeset	buses
нagat	things
нasharaat	insects

(c) *the collective plural*

Strictly speaking this is a third form of certain nouns (together with the singular and plural). It is used to describe a whole class of items collectively and generally, for example:

mooz	bananas
bortoo'aan	oranges

The collective form is extremely useful for the tourist since it mainly concerns food. In particular, it is more widely used than either the singular or the standard plural for all fruits and vegetables. For this reason it is always shown under those headings in the Arabic-English section of this book as the form you are most likely to hear or read.

The singular can be formed from the collective by the addition of **-a**. For example:

collective	**batikh**	water melon *or* water melons
sing.	**batikha**	a water melon
plural	**talaat batikhaat**	three water melons

The word **bisella** (peas), on the other hand, is only likely to occur in the collective form.

Further examples of the collective form are:

bayd	eggs
samak	fish
sha*r	hair
shuhgar	trees

IRREGULAR PLURALS

A large number of Arabic nouns have irregular plurals. Here is a list of relevant irregular plurals that a traveller might commonly need to use.

sing.	plural		sing.	plural	
shanta	**shōnuht**	bag(s)	**ism**	**asēmee**	name(s)
bank	**binook**	bank(s)	**maktab**	**makētib**	office(s)
sireer	**sarayir**	bed(s)	**ōda**	**ewuhd**	room(s)
kitab	**kutub**	book(s)	**taabe*a**	**tawaabe*a**	stamp(s)
walad	**owlad**	boy(s)	**shari*a**	**shawēri*a**	street(s)
akh	**ekhwāt**	brother(s)	**taalib**	**tuhluhbba**	student(s)
gamal	**gimal**	camel(s)	**tazkara**	**tazēkir**	ticket(s)
sigara	**saggayar**	cigarette(s)	**medeena**	**modon**	town(s)
yum	**ıyēm**	day(s)	**atr**	**otora**	train(s)
saнib	**asнaab**	friend(s)	**isboo*a**	**asabee*a**	week(s)
bint	**banat**	girl(s)			
fondō'	**fanādi'**	hotel(s)			
bayt	**beeyoot**	house(s)			
muftaн	**mafateeн**	key(s)			
raagil	**rigālla**	man (man)			
di'ee'a	**da'ay'**	minute(s)			
shahr	**shihor**	month(s)			
gāmi*a	**gawēmi*a**	mosque(s)			
matнaf	**matēнif**	museum(s)			

ARTICLES

THE DEFINITE ARTICLE (THE)
The definite article is **el**. It precedes the noun and remains unchanged whether the noun is masculine, feminine, singular or plural.

However, in front of words beginning with the letters d, n, r, s, sh, t, z, and optionally g and k, the 'l' is assimilated and the initial consonant is lengthened during pronunciation. This is shown as **e-** so that the form of the original word remains obvious. For example:

el shams	⟶ **e-shams**	the sun
el raagil	⟶ **e-raagil**	the man

El may also be assimilated with several prepositions. For example:

bee/bi + el ⟶ **bil**	as in **bil atr** by train
fee/fi + el ⟶ **fil**	as in **fil baнr** in the sea **fil maya** per cent
lee/li + el ⟶ **lil**	as in **lil mattar** to the airport **lil balad** to town
***ala + el** ⟶ ***alel**	as in ***alel bilasн** on the beach

THE INDEFINITE ARTICLE (A, AN)
There is no indefinite article in Arabic. The noun stands alone. For example:

ōtōbees	means 'bus' or 'a bus'
***arabaya**	means 'car' or 'a car'
ōtōbeeset	means 'buses' or 'some buses'

ADJECTIVES

Adjectives follow the noun they describe and agree with the noun in gender and number, for example:

fondō' kwɪyis	a good hotel
akla kwɪyissa	a good meal

The feminine of adjectives is formed by adding **-a**, for example:

masculine	feminine
gameel **kebeer**	**gameela** **kebeera**

Occasionally the final consonant is doubled following a short vowel, for example:

masculine	feminine
kwɪyis	**kwɪyissa**

Adjectives ending in **-ee** are invariable and do not change their form whether they are used with masculine or feminine nouns, for example:

gurnaan ingileezee   an English newspaper
*arabaya ingileezee   an English car

Note that if you use 'very' with an adjective then the Arabic word for 'very' always follows the adjective it qualifies, for example:

akla kwıyissa awee   a very good meal

If the definite article is used then it must occur twice – once in front of the noun and once in front of any adjective that goes with the noun, for example:

el maнatta e-ra'eesaya   the main station
e-raagil el *agooz   the old man
el 'consul' el breetaanee   the British Consul

ADJECTIVES AND PLURAL NOUNS
(a) If a plural noun, masculine or feminine, refers to humans then a plural adjective must be used. This can be formed by adding **-een** to the singular adjective, for example:

sing.   plural
kwıyis   **kwıyiseen**
nas kwıyiseen   nice people

(b) If a plural noun refers to inanimate objects then the adjective takes the feminine singular form (regardless of the gender of the original noun), for example:

feminine   **mabēnee kebeera**   large buildings
masculine   **fanadi' kebeera**   large hotels

(c) A dual plural noun should always be followed by a plural adjective, for example:

mabnayayn kubaar   two large buildings

IRREGULAR PLURAL ADJECTIVES
Many plural adjectives are irregular. Here is a list of the commoner ones:

sing.	plural	
kebeer	**kubaar**	large
sooghıyar	**sooghaar**	small
shedeed	**shudād**	strong
rakhees	**rokhaas**	cheap
adeem	**odam**	old (*not used for people*)
gameel	**goomal**	beautiful
nedeef	**nudaf**	clean

COMPARATIVES AND SUPERLATIVES (BIGGER, BIGGEST etc)
The comparative and superlative forms of the adjective are the same. They also remain the same for either sex or number.

Common comparative and superlative adjectives are:

ADJ	COMP/SUPER	
kebeer	akbar	bigger/biggest
sooghıyar	uhsgar	smaller/smallest
ghēlee	eghla	more/most expensive
rekhees	arkhuhs	cheaper/cheapest
gameel	agmal	more/most beautiful
Helw	aнla	nicer/nicest; prettier/prettiest
kwıyis	aнsen	better/best
keteer	aktar	more/most

For example:

fondō' akbar   a bigger hotel
el fondō' el akbar   the bigger/biggest hotel

To compare two things in Arabic you simply use the comparative form of the adjective + **min**, for example:

akbar min
bigger than

el kaheera akbar min el lu'sor
Cairo is bigger than Luxor

To express a superlative meaning you simply reverse the word order, i.e.:

comparative adjective + noun (without the article)

For example:

akbar haram   the biggest pyramid
aнsen fondō'   the best hotel

DEMONSTRATIVE ADJECTIVES (THIS, THAT, THESE, THOSE)
The demonstrative adjectives are:

da	*(masculine singular)*	this/that
dee	*(feminine singular)*	this/that
dol	*(masc. and fem. plurals)*	these/those

They follow **el** + noun, for example:

e-raagil da   this/that man
el bint dee   this/that girl
e-nas dol   these/those people

POSSESSIVE ADJECTIVES (MY, YOUR etc)
There are no possessive adjectives as in English. Instead, Arabic adds suffixes to the noun. They are added directly to a masculine noun or to the construct form of a feminine noun, where the **-a** has been replaced by **-it** (see page 99).

The suffix varies according to the number or gender of the possessor, for example:

noun + **ee**	my
noun + **ak**	your (*masc. sing.*)
noun + **ik**	your (*fem. sing.*)
noun + **oo**	his
noun + **ha**	her
noun + **na**	our
noun + **koo**	your (*plural*)
noun + **hum**	their

shantitee	my bag
umak	your mother (*said to a man*)
umik	your mother (*said to a woman*)
baytna	our house
***ınwānhum**	their address

Possession can also be shown by using **bita*** (of). This must also be made to agree in gender and number with the possessor, as above. It also varies with the gender of the thing which is possessed.

object masculine	*object feminine*	
bita*ee	bita*tee	my
bita*ak	bita*tak	your (*owner masculine*)
bita*ik	bita*tik	your (*owner feminine*)
bita*oo	bita*too	his
bita*ha	bita*t-ha	her
bita*ana	bita*tna	our
bita*akoo	bita*tkoo	your
bita*ahum	bita*t-hum	their

The word **bita*** follows the noun and requires the definite article **el** in front of the noun, for example:

e-shanta bita*tee	my bag
el bayt bita*ee	my house

Note that **bita*** should not be used for people. For example, to say 'my brother' you must use the suffix form of the possessive.

But **bita*** should always be used with any word that has been borrowed from another language. These words often appear in the text of this book in inverted commas, for example:

el 'camera' bita*tee	my camera

PRONOUNS

PERSONAL PRONOUNS

Personal pronouns which replace the subject of a sentence (I, you etc) exist in Arabic as independent words. Personal pronouns functioning as a direct object (me, you etc) or as an indirect object (to me, to you etc) take the form of suffixes to the verb. Here is a list of personal pronouns.

SUBJECT		DIRECT OBJECT		INDIRECT OBJECT	
ana	I	verb +**nee**	me	verb + **nee**	to me
inta	you (*m*)	verb + **ak**	you (*m*)	verb + **lak**	to you (*m*)
intee	you (*f*)	verb + **ik**	you (*f*)	verb + **lik**	to you (*f*)
hoowa	he/it	verb + **oo**	him/it	verb + **loo**	to him/it
haya	she/it	verb + **ha**	her/it	verb + **lha**	to her/it
eнna	we	verb + **na**	us	verb + **lna**	to us
intoo	you (*pl*)	verb + **koo**	you (*pl*)	verb + **lkoo**	to you (*pl*)
humma	they	verb + **hum**	them	verb + **lahum**	to them

sibtaha hena
I left it here   (*object feminine*)

sibtoo hena
I left it here   (*object masculine*)

shuftuhum e-naharda e-subн
I saw them this morning

Note that in Arabic subject pronouns may be omitted when the conjugation of the verb makes them superfluous. **Ana** (I) is the most likely to be omitted, as in the examples above.

When a sentence contains both direct and indirect objects the order will be the same as in English, i.e. verb + direct object + indirect object, for example:

eddeehanee!   give it to me!

REFLEXIVE PRONOUNS (MYSELF, YOURSELF etc)
Reflexive pronouns are:

nafsee	myself
nafsak	yourself (*masculine sing.*)
nafsik	yourself (*feminine sing.*)
nafsoo	himself
nafsaha	herself
nafsinna	ourselves
nafsukoo	yourselves
nafsoohu	themselves

a*miloo binafsak   do it yourself

USE OF PRONOUNS WITH PREPOSITIONS
Pronouns frequently occur suffixed to prepositions. They then follow a set pattern depending on whether the preposition ends with a vowel or a consonant, for example:

*alashēn (for)   **ma*a** (with)

*alashen-ee	for me	ma*a-ya	with me
-ak	for you (*masc.*)	-k	with you (*masc.*)
-ik	for you (*fem.*)	-ki	with you (*fem.*)
-oo	for him	-h	with him
-ha	for her	-ha	with her
-na	for us	-na	with us
-koo	for you (*pl.*)	-koo	with you (*pl.*)
-hum	for them	-hum	with them

The same endings can be used with these words:

min (from)   **zay** (like)   ***ala** (on/against)

da minee   that's from me
haya zayik   she's like you
da *alashenna?   is that for us?

You will often find them used in very colloquial phrases, for example:

ma*ak kabreet?   have you got any matches?
            (literally: matches with you?)

In fact, ***and** (at) + suffixed pronoun is even used in place of the verb 'to have' – which does not exist in Arabic. See page 114.

DEMONSTRATIVE PRONOUNS (THIS, THAT, THESE, THOSE)
The demonstrative pronouns are the same as the demonstrative adjectives:

da	(*masculine singular*)	this/that
dee	(*feminine singular*)	this/that
dol	(*masc. and fem. plural*)	these/those

They must agree in number and gender with the noun they are replacing and precede it in a sentence (as in English), for example:

da fondō' kwɪyis   that's a good hotel
dee *arabeetee   that's my car
mumkin dee/da?   can I have that one?
dee/da aнsen   that's better

Where gender is unspecified, as in the last examples above, then either **dee** or **da** may be used although the feminine **dee** is probably the more likely.

POSSESSIVE PRONOUNS (MINE, YOURS etc)

These are the same as the suffixed forms of **bita*** which can be used in place of possessive adjectives.

object masculine   *object feminine*

bita*ee	bita*tee	mine
bita*ak	bita*tak	yours (*owner masculine*)
bita*ik	bita*tik	yours (*owner feminine*)
bita*oo	bita*too	his
bita*ha	bita*t-ha	hers
bita*ana	bita*tna	ours
bita*akoo	bita*tkoo	yours
bita*ahum	bita*t-hum	theirs

e-shanta bita*tee	the bag's mine
da bita*ee!	that's mine!

Note that the first example could also mean 'my bag'.

OF

Phrases such as 'the address of the hotel' are expressed as follows:

noun (possessed) + el + noun (possessor)

For example:

*ınwān el fondō'	the address of the hotel
wa't e-reнla	the time of the flight
ism e-shari*a	the name of the street

Feminine nouns (as the possessed) appear in the construct form (**-a** becomes **-it**, see page 99), for example:

shantit el bint	the girl's handbag
odit bintee	my daughter's room

To make the phrase indefinite simply omit the article, for example:

нettit *ı-esh	a piece of bread
kubbayit shay	a cup of tea

The rule is the same with proper nouns, for example:

bayt aнmad	Ahmed's house
medeenit el iskindraya	the city of Alexandria

VERBS

THE INFINITIVE (TO LIKE, TO EAT etc)
There is no infinitive in Arabic. Instead, the verb is recognized by the form taken by the 3rd person singular in the perfect tense. This form is shown in column 1 of the table of Arabic verbs below, for example:

Habb he liked   **kal** he ate

This is how Arabic verbs are represented in dictionaries and the English-Arabic section of this book follows this convention.

When translating English sentences containing an infinitive, both verbs must agree with the subject. For example:

*a-ızeen nerooн lee ...   we want to go to ...
                                      (literally: we want we go to ...)

TABLE OF COMMON ARABIC VERBS
This table shows the two Arabic tenses in the first person singular, or 'I' form, which is the form you are most likely to need in conversation.

1 Infinitive equivalent ('he' form, perfect tense)	2 'I' form IMPERFECT	3 'I' form PERFECT	
sa'al	as'al	sa'alt	to ask
		kunt	to be †
aydir	a'dar	aydirt	to be able to
beda'a	abda	beda'at	to begin
gab	ageeb	gibt	to bring
ishtera	ashteree	ishtereet	to buy
ga	agee	gayt	to come †
shirib	ashrab	shribt	to drink
kal	akul	kalt	to eat
edda	addee	idayt	to give
raн	arooн	roнt	to go †
	*andee		to have †
*arif	a*aruhf	*arift	to know
нabb	aнebb	нabbayt	to like/love
buhss	aboss	buhseet	to look
*amal	a*mil	*amalt	to make/do
нuhtt	aнott	нattayt	to put
al	a'ool	olt	to say/tell
shuf	ashoof	shuft	to see
nam	anām	nimt	to sleep
kallim	atkallim	kallimt	to speak
khad	akhud	khat	to take
fakar	afakuhr	fakart	to think
fehim	afham	fehimt	to understand †
mishee	imshee	misheet	to walk, go away
	*a-ıyiz		to want †
ishtaghel	ashtaghel	ishtaghelt	to work

† see page 113-115

TENSES

Strictly speaking there are only two tenses of the verb: the imperfect (used for incomplete action in the *present* or the *future*) and the perfect (for completed action in the *past*).

However, colloquial Egyptian Arabic can make a distinction between present and future usage of the imperfect tense by the addition of extra prefixes (see below).

IMPERFECT TENSE

The imperfect tense is formed by adding prefixes and suffixes to a verb stem. You can work out the stem by removing the initial **a** from the 'I' form in column 2 of the verb table above. For example:

aнebb gives the stem **нebb**

The verb is conjugated by adding the following prefixes and suffixes to the stem:

a____	aнebb	I like
ti____	tiнebb	you like (*masc. sing.*)
ti____ee	tiнebbee	you like (*fem. sing.*)
yi____	yiнebb	he likes
ti____	tiнebb	she likes
ni____	niнebb	we like
ti____oo	tiнebboo	you like (*plural*)
yi____oo	yiнebboo	they like

In practice and in this book, you may find the first vowel is pronounced or transliterated as **e** or **i** in different verbs, depending on the actual sound of the word. However, the grammatical process is constant.

PRESENT USAGE OF THE IMPERFECT TENSE

The imperfect conjugation can be used for the present tense. In colloquial Egyptian Arabic the prefix **bi-** is added to the imperfect tense to make it clear that the action of a verb is in the present, for example:

baнebb †	I like
bitнebb	you like (*masc. sing.*)
bitнebbee	you like (*fem. sing.*)
biнebb	he likes
bitнebb	she likes
binнebb	we like
bitнebboo	you like (*plural*)
biнebboo	they like

† The **i** is not heard here in spoken Arabic.

Note the elision of the second vowel in typical native speech where **bitiнebb** becomes **bitнebb**. If you neglect to do this you will still be understood.

FUTURE USAGE OF THE IMPERFECT TENSE (I WILL, YOU WILL etc)

The imperfect tense can also be modified to show that the action will occur in the future by adding the prefix **на-** to the stem, for example:

наНebb	I will like
наtНebb	you will like (*masc. sing*)
наtНebbee	you will like (*fem. sing.*)
НІНebb †	he will like
наtНebb	she will like
нанНebb	we will like
наtНebboo	you will like (*plural*)
НІНebboo †	they will like

† The sound changes in spoken Arabic.

PERFECT TENSE (I ATE, I HAVE EATEN etc)
The perfect tense is used for completed action in the past. It is used for both the simple past and the perfect tense in English. For example:

ana shuftoo   translates as   I saw him/I have seen him

The perfect tense is formed by adding suffixes to a verb stem (except in the case of the third person masculine singular 'he'). To find the stem, remove the final **t** from the verb form shown in column 3 of the verb table on page 109. For example **kallim** is the perfect stem for the verb 'to speak'.

For the third person masculine or 'he' form, use the word in column 1 of the verb table (page 109) (or the first translation in the English-Arabic section of this book).

Most verbs are conjugated as follows:

-t	kallimt	I spoke/have spoken
-t	kallimt	you spoke/have spoken (*masc. sing.*)
-tee	kallimtee	you spoke/have spoken (*fem. sing.*)
-	kallim	he spoke/has spoken
-it	kallimit	she spoke/has spoken
-na	kallimna	we spoke/have spoken
-too	kallimtoo	you spoke/have spoken (*plural*)
-oo	kallimoo	they spoke/have spoken

Exceptions

(a) to give, to like, to put. For these verbs, remove **-ayt** from the word in column 3 (page 109) to find the stem and then add the following suffixes:

-ayt	idayt	I gave/have given
-ayt	idayt	you gave/have given (*masc. sing.*)
-aytee	idaytee	you gave/have given (*fem. sing.*)
-	edda	he gave/has given
-it	idit	she gave/has given
-ayna	idayna	we have/have given
-aytoo	idaytoo	you gave/have given (*plural*)
-oo	idoo	they gave/have given

(b) to buy, to look, to go away. For these verbs, remove **-eet** from the word in column 3 (page 109) to find the stem and then add the following suffixes:

-eet	ishtereet	I bought/have bought
-eet	ishtereet	you bought/have bought (*masc. sing.*)
-eetee	ishtereetee	you bought/have bought (*fem. sing.*)
-	ishtera	he bought/has bought
-it	ishterit	she bought/has bought
-eena	ishtereena	we bought/have bought
-eetoo	ishtereetoo	you bought/have bought (*plural*)
-oo	ishteroo	they bought/have bought

MAKING THE VERB NEGATIVE

The negative is formed by joining **ma** to the front of the verb and adding **sh** to the end, for example:

mabadakhansh	I don't smoke
ma*andeesh	I haven't got

This can sometimes result in a very long word. If you find this difficult to form at first, another way of making a verb negative is by using the word **mush** in front of the verb, for example:

mush *aruhf	I don't know
or **ma*arafsh**	

There are a few 'verbs' which only use the **mush** version of the negative. These include 'to want' and the alternative forms taken in the present by 'to go', 'to come' and 'to understand'.

mush *a-ıyiz нaga	I don't want anything
mush fehim	I don't understand

THE IMPERATIVE (GIVING COMMANDS)

To form an imperative omit the initial **t** from the second person singular or plural of the verb in the imperfect tense, for example:

eshrab!	drink up!
eddeehanee	give it to me

Some other useful imperatives are:

estanna hena	stay here
imshee!	go away!
o'af!	stop!
ta*ala hena	come here

To form the negative imperative (don't ...) take the second person singular or plural of the verb in the imperfect tense and add **ma-** at the front and **-sh** at the end, for example:

mato'afsh!	don't stop!
matestannash	don't wait

QUESTIONS
In Arabic the word order of a question is identical to that of the corresponding statement, for example:

inta *a-ɪyiz нaga	you want something
inta *a-ɪyiz нaga?	do you want something?

The difference is marked by using the same intonation at the end as you would in an English question.

INTERROGATIVE WORDS
Words such as:

fayn?	where?	**lay?**	why?
emta?	when?	**izzay?**	how?

are usually placed at the end of a question. They do, however, also occur at the beginning, sometimes for emphasis, for example:

el maнatta fayn?	where is the station?
or **fayn el maнatta?**	

IRREGULAR VERBS
There are very few irregular verbs in Arabic. However there are several words used in a verbal sense which are not 'grammatically' verbs at all. These exceptional cases, which all translate into very common verbs in English, are given below.

TO BE
There is no equivalent to the present tense of the verb 'to be' (am/is/are) in Arabic.

Simple sentences in which forms of the verb 'to be' occur do not require a verb in Arabic. Some examples follow:

tazkartak fayn?	where is your ticket?
e-gow gameel e-naharda	the weather's lovely today
ana mabsoot awee	I'm very happy
el mat*am da kwɪyis?	is this restaurant any good?

In the past tense the verb 'to be' is conjugated as follows:

ana kunt	I was
inta kunt	you were (*masc. sing.*)
intee kuntee	you were (*fem. sing.*)
hoowa kan	he was
haya kanit	she was
eнna kunna	we were
intoo kuntoo	you were (*plural*)
humma kanoo	they were

For example:

kunt fayn?	where were you?

Negatives are formed in the standard way:

ana makuntish	I wasn't
hoowa makansh	he wasn't
etc	

Note also:

fee	there is/are
mafeesh	there isn't/aren't
kan fee	there was/were
makansh fee	there wasn't/weren't

TO HAVE

The preposition ***and** is used with the appropriate suffixes:

*andee	I have
*andak	you have (*masc. sing.*)
*andik	you have (*fem. sing.*)
*andoo	he has
*andaha	she has
*andenna	we have
*andukoo	you have (*plural*)
*anduhum	they have

The future tense is formed by placing the word ** HIkoon** in front of the word for 'have', for example:

HIkoon *andak   you will have

The past tense is formed by placing **kan** in front, for example:

kan *andak   you had

TO WANT

(a) present tense

In the present tense all singular forms are represented by:

*a-IYiz   (*if subject masculine*)
*a-IZa   (*if subject feminine*)

All plural forms are represented by:

*a-IZeen

Negatives are formed by placing **mush** in front, for example:

mush *a-IYiz   I don't want (to), he doesn't want (to)

(b) the past tense

kunt *a-IYiz	I wanted (*masc.*)
kunt *a-IZa	I wanted (*fem.*)
kunt *a-IYiz	you wanted (*masc.*)
kuntee *a-IZa	you wanted (*fem.*)
kan *a-IYiz	he wanted
kanit *a-IZa	she wanted
kunna *a-IZeen	we wanted
kuntoo *a-IZeen	you wanted (*plural*)
kanoo *a-IZeen	they wanted

The negative is formed thus:

makuntish *a-ıyiz	I didn't want (to)
makansh *a-ıyiz	he didn't want (to)

TO COME, TO GO, TO UNDERSTAND

As alternatives to the present tense of these verbs the following participles are frequently used. Although they are not actually 'verbs', they have verbal meaning:

	come	go	understand
all masc. sing. forms	**gay**	**гıaн**	**fēhim**
all fem. sing. forms	**gaya**	**гıнa**	**fēhma**
all plural forms	**gayeen**	**гıнeen**	**fēhmeen**

For example:

ana гıaн	I'm going
inta gay?	are you coming?

To make these negative place **mush** in front of the participle, for example:

ana mush гıaн	I'm not going

TELLING THE TIME

what time is it?	e-sa*a kam?
it is ...	'it is' does not occur on its own in Egyptian Arabic
(it is) one o'clock	e-sa*a waнda
(it is) seven o'clock	e-sa*a sab*a
one a.m.	e-sa*a waнda e-subн
seven a.m.	e-sa*a sab*a e-subн
one p.m.	e-sa*a waнda ba*d e-dohr (ba*d e-dohr means 'in the afternoon')
seven p.m.	e-sa*a sab*a bil layl (bil layl means 'in the evening')
midday	e-dohr
midnight	nus el layl
five past eight	e-sa*a tamania wi khamsa
five to eight	e-sa*a tamania illa khamsa
half past ten	e-sa*a *ashara wi nus
quarter past eleven	e-sa*a нidaashar wi rub*a
quarter to eleven	e-sa*a нidaashar illa rub*a
five past	wi khamsa
ten past	wi *ashara
quarter past	wi rub*a
twenty past	wi tilt
twenty five past	wi nus illa khamsa
half past	wi nus
twenty five to	wi nus wi khamsa
twenty to	illa tilt
quarter to	illa rub*a
ten to	illa *ashara
five to	illa khamsa

CONVERSION TABLES

1. LENGTH

centimetres, centimeters
1 cm = 0.39 inches

metres, meters
1 m = 100 cm = 1000 mm
1 m = 39.37 inches = 1.09 yards

kilometres, kilometers
1 km = 1000 m
1 km = 0.62 miles = 5/8 mile

km	1	2	3	4	5	10	20	30	40	50	100
miles	0.6	1.2	1.9	2.5	3.1	6.2	12.4	18.6	24.9	31.1	62.1

inches
1 inch = 2.54 cm

feet
1 foot = 30.48 cm

yards
1 yard = 0.91 m

miles
1 mile = 1.61 km = 8/5 km

miles	1	2	3	4	5	10	20	30	40	50	100
km	1.6	3.2	4.8	6.4	8.0	16.1	32.2	48.3	64.4	80.5	161

2. WEIGHT

gram(me)s
1 g = 0.035 oz

g	100	250	500
oz	3.5	8.75	17.5 = 1.1 lb

kilos
1 kg = 1000 g
1 kg = 2.20 lb = 11/5 lb

kg	0.5	1	1.5	2	3	4	5	6	7	8	9	10
lb	1.1	2.2	3.3	4.4	6.6	8.8	11.0	13.2	15.4	17.6	19.8	22

kg	20	30	40	50	60	70	80	90	100
lb	44	66	88	110	132	154	176	198	220

tons
1 UK ton = 1018 kg
1 US ton = 909 kg

tonnes
1 tonne = 1000 kg
1 tonne = 0.98 UK tons = 1.10 US tons

ounces
1 oz = 28.35 g

pounds
1 pound = 0.45 kg = 5/11 kg

lb	1	1.5	2	3	4	5	6	7	8	9	10	20
kg	0.5	0.7	0.9	1.4	1.8	2.3	2.7	3.2	3.6	4.1	4.5	9.1

stones
1 stone = 6.35 kg

stones	1	2	3	7	8	9	10	11	12	13	14	15
kg	6.3	12.7	19	44	51	57	63	70	76	83	89	95

hundredweights
1 UK hundredweight = 50.8 kg
1 US hundredweight = 45.36 kg

3. CAPACITY

litres, liters
1 l = 1.76 UK pints = 2.13 US pints
$\frac{1}{2}$ l = 500 cl
$\frac{1}{4}$ l = 250 cl

pints
1 UK pint = 0.57 l
1 US pint = 0.47 l

quarts
1 UK quart = 1.14 l
1 US quart = 0.95 l

gallons
1 UK gallon = 4.55 l
1 US gallon = 3.79 l

4. TEMPERATURE

centigrade/Celsius
$C = (F - 32) \times 5/9$

C	−5	0	5	10	15	18	20	25	30	37	38
F	23	32	41	50	59	64	68	77	86	98.4	100.4

Fahrenheit
$F = (C \times 9/5) + 32$

F	23	32	40	50	60	65	70	80	85	98.4	101
C	−5	0	4	10	16	20	21	27	30	37	38.3

NUMBERS

•	0	sifr
١	1	waaHid; *(for feminine nouns)* waHda
٢	2	itneen
٣	3	talaata
٤	4	arba*a
٥	5	khamsa
٦	6	sitta
٧	7	sab*a
٨	8	tamania
٩	9	tis*a
١٠	10	*ashara
١١	11	Hidaashar
١٢	12	itnaashar
١٣	13	talattaashar
١٤	14	arba*taashar
١٥	15	khamastaashar
١٦	16	sittaashar
١٧	17	saba*taashar
١٨	18	tamantaashar
١٩	19	tisa*taashar
٢٠	20	*ashreen
٢١	21	waaHid wa *ashreen
٢٢	22	itneen wa *ashreen
٢٣	23	talaata wa *ashreen
٢٤	24	arba*a wa *ashreen
٢٥	25	khamsa wa *ashreen
٢٦	26	sitta wa *ashreen
٢٧	27	sab*a wa *ashreen
٢٨	28	tamania wa *ashreen
٢٩	29	tis*a wa *ashreen
٣٠	30	talateen
٣١	31	waaHid wi talateen
٣٢	32	itneen wi talateen
٤٠	40	arba*een
٤١	41	waaHid wa arba*een
٥٠	50	khamseen

٥١	51	waaHid wi khamseen
٦٠	60	sitteen
٧٠	70	sab*een
٨٠	80	tamaneen
٩٠	90	tis*een
١٠٠	100	maya
١٠١	101	maya waaHid
١٠٢	102	maya witneen
١٠٣	103	maya wi talaata
١٠٤	104	maya warba*a
١٠٥	105	maya wi khamsa
٢٠٠	200	mitayn
٣٠٠	300	tultoomaya
٤٠٠	400	rub*amaya
٥٠٠	500	khumsoomaya
٦٠٠	600	sittoomaya
٧٠٠	700	sub*amaya
٨٠٠	800	tomnoomaya
٩٠٠	900	tis*a-oomaya
١٠٠٠	1000	alf
٢٠٠٠	2000	alfayn
٣٠٠٠	3000	talaat talef
٤٠٠٠	4000	arba* talef
١٩٨٨	1988	alf tis*a-oomaya tamania wi tamaneen

	masculine	feminine
1st	*el owel*	*el oola*
2nd	*e-tanee*	*e-tania*
3rd	*e-taalet*	*e-talta*
4th	*e-rabia**	*e-raba**
5th	*el khamis*	*el khamsa*
6th	*es-saddis*	*es-sadsa*
7th	*es-sabia**	*es-saba*a*
8th	*e-tamen*	*e-tamna*
9th	*e-tassia**	*e-tassa*a*
10th	*el *asher*	*el *ashara*